Simply Effective CBT Supervi

CBT is the most widely endorsed Evidence Based Treatment (EBT) for psychological disorders. This innovative volume exclusively addresses CBT supervision, which plays a vital role in the translation of CBT from an EBT to routine practice.

Supervision requires a combination of knowledge and skill – the knowledge of the appropriate CBT protocol for the situation and the skill to equip the practitioner with the competencies to deliver these protocols in the context in which they are operating. In *Simply Effective CBT Supervision*, Michael J. Scott provides a unique guide to the particular skills necessary to monitor the fidelity and competence with which an EBT is implemented. There is an emphasis throughout on the importance of experiential learning, with detailed transcripts of supervisor–supervisee conversations, a focus on group supervision and the management of group processes. The power differential between supervisor and supervisee is acknowledged and addressed with guidelines and safeguards that will ensure that client needs can be addressed in a spirit of collaborative empiricism, and the text also covers the importance of matching the supervisor and supervisee.Downloadable worksheets for supervisor and supervisee are available on the book's eResources website.

Covering the skills necessary to be an effective CBT supervisor, this is the ideal book for current and prospective CBT supervisors looking to extend their knowledge base.

Michael J. Scott is a consultant psychologist working in Liverpool. His previous books in this series are *Simply Effective Group CBT* and *Simply Effective CBT*, and he is the author of seven other titles including *CBT for Common Trauma Responses* and *Moving on after Trauma*. Dr Scott is currently an external examiner at Sheffield Hallam University, UK.

Simply Effective CBT Supervision

Michael J. Scott

Routledge
Taylor & Francis Group

LONDON AND NEW YORK

First published 2014
by Routledge
27 Church Road, Hove, East Sussex, BN3 2FA

and by Routledge
711 Third Avenue, New York, NY 10017

Routledge is an imprint of the Taylor & Francis Group, an informa business

© 2014 Michael J. Scott

British Library Cataloguing in Publication Data
A catalogue record for this book is available from the British Library

Library of Congress Cataloging in Publication Data
Scott, Michael J., 1948–
Simply effective CBT supervision / Michael J. Scott.
pages cm
ISBN 978-0-415-53954-8 (hardback) – ISBN 978-0-415-53955-5 (pbk.)
– ISBN 978-1-31587980-2 (ebook)—1. Psychotherapy.—2.
Psychotherapists–Supervison of.—3. Clinical competence.—I. Title.
RC480.5.S375 2014
616.89'14–dc23

2013025353

ISBN: 978–0–415–53954–8 (hbk)
ISBN: 978–0–415–53955–5 (pbk)
ISBN: 978–1–315–87980–2 (ebk)

Typeset in Times New Roman
by RefineCatch Limited, Bungay, Suffolk

Please visit the eResources website at
www.routledge.com/9780415539555

Printed and bound in the United States of America by Publishers Graphics,
LLC on sustainably sourced paper.

Simply Effective CBT Supervision

Michael J. Scott

LONDON AND NEW YORK

First published 2014
by Routledge
27 Church Road, Hove, East Sussex, BN3 2FA

and by Routledge
711 Third Avenue, New York, NY 10017

Routledge is an imprint of the Taylor & Francis Group, an informa business

© 2014 Michael J. Scott

British Library Cataloguing in Publication Data
A catalogue record for this book is available from the British Library

Library of Congress Cataloging in Publication Data
Scott, Michael J., 1948–
Simply effective CBT supervision / Michael J. Scott.
pages cm
ISBN 978-0-415-53954-8 (hardback) – ISBN 978-0-415-53955-5 (pbk.)
– ISBN 978-1-31587980-2 (ebook)—1. Psychotherapy.—2.
Psychotherapists–Supervison of.—3. Clinical competence.—I. Title.
RC480.5.S375 2014
616.89'14–dc23

2013025353

ISBN: 978–0–415–53954–8 (hbk)
ISBN: 978–0–415–53955–5 (pbk)
ISBN: 978–1–315–87980–2 (ebk)

Typeset in Times New Roman
by RefineCatch Limited, Bungay, Suffolk

Please visit the eResources website at
www.routledge.com/9780415539555

Printed and bound in the United States of America by Publishers Graphics,
LLC on sustainably sourced paper.

Contents

Figures

Tables

Acknowledgements

Table 5.1 was originally published in C. Ecclestone, S. Morley and A. C. Williams, 'Review: Limited evidence that psychological therapies are of benefit for adults with chronic pain', *Evidence-based Mental Health*, Vol. 12, No. 4, p. 118 (2009). It appears here by kind permission of the BMJ Publishing Group Ltd.

Table 11.2 and Appendix F were originally published in M. Palomo, H. Beinart and M. Cooper, 'Development and validation of the Supervisory Relationship Questionnaire (SRQ) in UK trainee clinical psychologists', *British Journal of Clinical Psychology*, Vol. 49, No. 2, pp. 131–49 (2010). They appear here by kind permission of Wiley.

Table 11.3 was originally published in P. Kenneth Gordon, 'Ten steps to cognitive behavioural supervision', *The Cognitive Behaviour Therapist*, Vol. 5, pp. 71–82 (2012). It appears here by kind permission of P. K. Gordon and Cambridge University Press.

Appendix A was originally published in G. Sloan, 'Clinical supervision: Beginning the supervisory relationship', *British Journal of Nursing*, Vol. 14, No. 17, pp. 918–23 (2005). It appears here by kind permission of the British Psychological Society.

Appendix C was originally published in D. L. Hollon and S. D. Chambless, 'Defining empirically supported therapies', *Journal of Consulting and Clinical Psychology*, Vol. 66, No. 1, pp. 7–18 (1998).

Chapter 1

Supervision past, present and future

This chapter tracks the evolution of CBT supervision from its roots in traditional generic supervision to its contemporary mandate to translate and disseminate efficacious treatments into effective treatments in routine practice. The chapter begins by detailing the ways in which CBT supervision is similar to generic supervision and how, to a degree, both mirror treatment. However, CBT supervision can be distinguished from generic supervision by the former's appeal to a mediational model, in which responses to stimuli are mediated by cognition. The focus of the next section is then on the cognitive model of human behaviour. Within CBT 'cognitions' can be conceptualised differently and this has led to a variety of treatments, and the following section indicates that a different expertise (a particular set of knowledge and skills) is required of a supervisor for the different modalities sheltering under the CBT umbrella. Despite these differences there is a common structure to all CBT supervision sessions and this is elaborated next. Whilst there has been much theorising about what constitutes good CBT supervision and supervision in general, there are important question marks about whether, as currently practised, supervision positively affects client outcomes in routine practise and this issue is addressed next. This is followed by a focus on the practical difficulties of a supervisee acquiring a credible supervisor. In the context of a 'not proven' verdict about traditional CBT supervision, a revised model of CBT supervision is presented in which the supervisor is viewed as a conduit for evidence-based treatments. In turn this re-conceptualisation leads to viewing front-line clinicians as tasked with delivering EBTs (Evidence Based Treatment). The penultimate section of this chapter therefore suggests that 'scientist practitioner' is a poor descriptor of the front-line clinician's daily practice and that they are more akin to 'engineers', whilst CBT therapists who are academic clinicians funded primarily by a university are 'scientists'. The biggest challenge facing CBT is dissemination and, as at the time of the industrial revolution, it is engineers who are poised to make the leaps forward. The cultures and needs of scientists and engineers are different, neither must be subservient to the other, but able to draw on each other's expertise, such that there is often a degree of overlap between scientists and engineers but they are substantially different. This new conceptualisation of supervision does not sit easily with a supervisee who wishes to 'pick and mix' amongst the CBT therapies or sees no value in diagnostic labels and these issues are addressed in the final section.

Commonalities between CBT supervision and generic supervision

CBT supervision draws on the components of generic supervision. Below is a typical generic pro-forma used by NHS Trusts in the UK:

Table 1.1 Generic template for monitoring the effectiveness of supervision

Was a supervision contract agreed at the beginning of the supervision period?	Yes	No
Is there a written record of supervision sessions?	Yes	No
During supervision in the last. . . . .(insert time period), I have:		
	Yes	No
Reflected on my practice		
Explored ways of working with particular service users		
Explored the dynamics between myself and service users		
Discussed the effect of my work on my own feelings		
Received constructive feedback on my work		
Felt validated and supported as an employee		
Reviewed my workload		
Discussed my professional development		
Had opportunities for learning new skills or developing existing ones		
Felt able to raise aspects of my work which I don't feel confident about		
Discussed my relationships with colleagues		
Supervision has helped me in the following ways:		
As part of my supervision I would have liked:		
Elements of supervision that have not been useful:		

Table 1.1 serves as a useful reminder of necessary components of supervision. Just as a client has to be 'safe' in therapy, so too a supervisee has to be 'safe' in supervision. Without safety the supervisee's learning is compromised and they may not feel free to volunteer their feelings or have an open dialogue with their supervisor. There is a power differential between the supervisor and supervisee and therefore personal boundaries need to be put in place such as proscribing an intimate/sexual relationship. Professional boundaries mean that the supervisee should not be treated as a client if they volunteer material suggestive of a problem, rather it should be dealt with in the context of the impact on the client.

The supervisor–supervisee relationship may be formalised by contracts; see Appendix A for an example contract (Sloan, 2005). Unfortunately, the need for such contracts only becomes readily apparent when something goes wrong, such as a supervisor disclosing to a Manager some information about the supervisee that is not simply about the latter's output. The supervisee may then believe that they can no longer trust the supervisor. But there should also ideally be a contract between the supervisor and the Organisation/Manager which also specifies the boundaries of confidentiality. The contracts can then be an important reference in any dispute or areas of concern. The supervisor has responsibilities not only to the supervisee but also to his/her funding body and unless there is clarity about how the dual responsibilities are to be discharged one or other party may well be aggrieved. Whilst the contracts do necessarily have a legalistic flavour, nevertheless they serve as an important reminder to all parties, of the framework they should be operating in and may have a preventative function.

It is important that supervisor and supervisee agree in advance that supervision sessions comprehensively cover all the supervisee's work, not just for example those cases that are going well. Having sessions videoed can act as some protection against selectivity, but the cases selected for scrutiny can themselves be selective.

Supervision a mirror of treatment?

There are undoubted similarities between supervision and the treatment of a client in that supervisees (like clients) inevitably have different levels of experience and education and both require a tailoring of supervision/treatment to their needs. For example one supervisee may have a psychodynamic/humanistic background, another may not; unwittingly in the former the supervisee is likely to raise issues like secondary gain which do not fit easily into a CBT framework and supervision will have to address this issue. In other instances there may be a major cultural/religious gap between supervisor and supervisee, just as there may be a similar gap between therapist and client; in both cases there is a need to understand the nuances of the assumptive world of the other. For the supervisor/therapist this may mean a need for dialogue with a colleague from the same culture/religion to avoid a stereotypical reaction.

Although CBT supervision has mirrored treatment there are important differences between them, see Table 1.2.

Supervision, outside of the context of training establishments, such as the Beck Institute, is not time limited; as such there is no beginning, middle and end. Because of the open-endedness of routine supervision it is probably easier for sessions to 'drift'. By contrast the novice therapist in time-limited supervision usually progresses from structured manualised treatments to a greater emphasis on formulation informed practice by the end of supervision, from a more didactic input from the supervisor initially to the therapist deciding on and evaluating therapeutic experiments, accompanied by reflective commentary from the supervisor.

Supervisees do not ordinarily present with an emotional disorder/problems in living as a prime focus, so whilst a supervisor may provide support in such

Table 1.2 Differences between supervision and treatment

1. Supervision is not usually of limited duration.
2. Supervisees do not present with readily identifiable 'deficits', in the way clients may present with specific disorders.
3. The focus of supervision with a supervisee is likely to be on a much wider range of disorders than the disorders suffered by any one client.
4. The focus of supervision is likely to range beyond any one CBT treatment modality.
5. It is assumed that a treating clinician has an expertise in treating the disorder that the client presents with but it is unlikely that the supervisor has an expertise in all the areas that might concern their supervisee.
6. The psychosocial environment of the supervisee will not usually significantly impair functioning in the way a client's does.
7. The supervisor and supervisee usually have a joint responsibility to a third party.

instances there would be a confusion of roles if the supervisor were to treat the supervisee. This is not to say that a supervisee may not have cognitions that interfere with the delivery of CBT and which would therefore become an appropriate focus in supervision. Common dysfunctional cognitions of novice therapists include: 'I shouldn't feel irritated by the client', 'I have got to get each session right', 'I must avoid making the client uncomfortable'. The first step is making these maladaptive attitudes explicit to the supervisee and the second step is re-appraising these attitudes by questioning, variously, their utility, the authority by which they are held and their validity. In some instances supervisees may be undergoing CBT supervision more as part of their job description rather than from a whole-hearted endorsement of CBT. Supervisees' reservations about CBT can include 'it's mechanistic', 'doesn't take proper account of historical material', 'leaves little room for emotion', 'people are more than computers'; such maladaptive attitudes need to be addressed in supervision if the full potency of CBT is to be released.

The breadth of discussions in supervision is likely to be much broader than the focal concerns in relation to any one client. The supervisor will inevitably have gaps in his knowledge base and limited practical experience of working with particular client groups but should be able to signpost the supervisee to suitable repositories of such knowledge and experience. Given the range of practice contexts of supervisees the supervisor will need to be able to go beyond Beckian cognitive therapy and should have at least a familiarity with other cognitive behaviour therapies, for example Self-instruction Training (Meichenbaum, 1985) – which would be more appropriate for a client with mild learning difficulties – or Problem Solving Therapy (Nezu and Nezu, 1989) for parasuicidal clients. Further, because of the need to disseminate CBT, it is incumbent on supervisors to acquaint themselves with low intensity interventions and group work to enable supervisees to advance these cost-effective modalities (see Scott, 2011).

What is distinctive about CBT supervision?

CBT supervision can be distinguished from other forms of supervision, in that it is based on the CBT philosophy of the reciprocal interactions of cognitions, behaviours, emotions and physiology, see Figure 1.1.

Thus a client's emotional state may be altered via any of the four ports of entry, cognition, emotion, behaviour or physiology in Figure 1.1, for example if the client was tense they might go for a walk, this would be an example of making a change via the physiology port. But Figure 1.1 also indicates that a client's emotional state is influenced by the climate that they are in, e.g. if the client has a highly critical partner this might dissuade them from going for a walk to unwind. For ease of illustration the climate is shown as operating via cognition, but in fact it exerts its effects through each of the four ports in the bottom part of Figure 1.1.

The therapist can also be thought of as operating via the climate in Figure 1.1, at some points in a treatment session acting via the cognitive port, when engaged in, say, Socratic dialogue with the client; at other times acting via the behavioural port when engaged in, perhaps, therapist-assisted exposure; in other sessions entering via the physiology port, with applied relaxation, for example. The ports of entry for the therapist are not meant to be mutually exclusive; for example, the

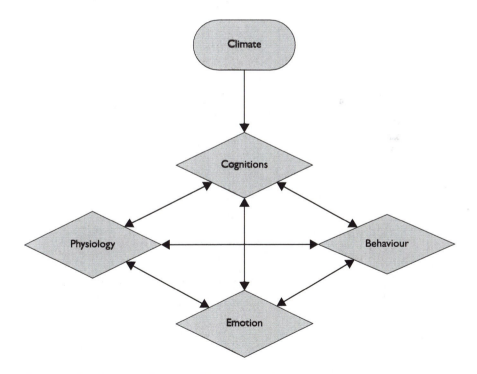

Figure 1.1 The Cognitive Behaviour Therapy model.

therapist might prepare the way cognitively for the replacement of one emotion, e.g. depression, with another emotion such as anger.

Both supervisor and supervisee exist in the climate cloud of Figure 1.1 and their experiential transactions can affect the client's emotional state below. However the client's emotional state can also affect the supervisee and usually indirectly the supervisor, see Figure 1.2.

The climate that exists between the supervisor and supervisee is, arguably, as important as the climate that exists between the therapist and client. It has been found that high levels of expressed emotion, i.e. of criticism and/or over involvement (Hooley *et al.*, 1986) exhibited by family members lead to relapse amongst clients who have recovered from depression. A 'toxic' climate between supervisor and supervisee may be similarly characterised by high levels of criticism and/or over involvement, leading to possible dsyfunctionality, though this is yet to be demonstrated empirically. It is suggested that effective supervision involves respecting the separate identity of the supervisee – that they are not just an extension of the supervisor and involved in a dependent relationship with him/her. Implicit in this is a recognition of boundaries – this is particularly important given the power differential between supervisor and supervisee. Further, criticism has to be constructive, confined to certain behaviours and thoughts and not a global attack on the supervisee. Thus CBT supervision is not simply about the supervisee acquiring technical skills any more than that CBT therapy is solely about the client learning specific techniques, such as how to use Thought Records. In this respect CBT supervision has commonalities with good practice supervision in other modalities.

The supervisor can better gauge a supervisee's functioning by using multiple sources of information, e.g. case discussion, role-play, video, and similarly the

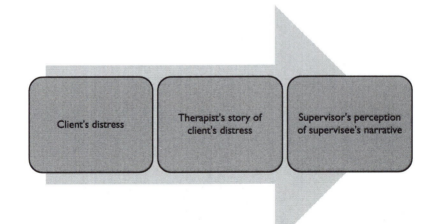

Figure 1.2 The translation of client distress to the supervisor.

teaching function of the supervisor should be multi-modal, e.g. modelling in role-play, directing reading, behavioural experiments. The range of foci of supervision should also be agreed in advance, e.g. diagnosis/problem specification, mastery of cognitive therapy methods, client–therapist relationship, therapist reactions and supervisory process.

CBT – A broad church

CBT therapies share a mediational model in that a person's responses to stimuli are believed to be effected by the cognitions (thoughts/images/meanings) attached to the stimuli. The CBT therapies are also psychoeducational in that they involve the teaching of skills. However, from the genesis of CBT in the 1960s there have been differences between the CBTs. For example Beckian (Beck *et al.*, 1979) cognitive therapy focuses on challenging the content of maladaptive thoughts, whilst in Metacognitive Therapy (MT) (Wells, 2009) the focus is on changing metacognitions, i.e. the thoughts about thoughts, and in Acceptance and Commitment Therapy (ACT) (Hayes *et al.*, 1999) clients are taught to 'just notice' previously unwanted thoughts/images and make commitments to goals that reflect the clients' values. The 'evolution' of the main CBTs is shown in Figure 1.3.

Each of the CBTs in Figure 1.3 has its own, relatively distinct, CBT protocols. Thus a supervisor may feel equipped to supervise a supervisee employing Beck's cognitive therapy but feel much less so to supervise a supervisee using Acceptance and Commitment Therapy (ACT). Some of the newer CBTs have been designed

First Wave 1960–1990

- Rational Emotive Therapy (RET) – Ellis (1962)
- Cognitive Therapy (CT) – Beck (1979)
- Stress Innoculation Training (SIT) – Meichenbaum (1985)
- Problem Solving Therapy (PST) – Nezu (1989)

Second Wave 1991–2000

- Dialectical Behaviour Therapy (DBT) – Linehan (1993)
- Schema Focussed Therapy (SFT) – Young (1994)
- Acceptance and Commitment Therapy (ACT) – Hayes (1999)

Third Wave 2000+

- Mindfulness Based Cognitive Therapy (MBT) – Segal (2002)
- Metacognitive Therapy (MT) – Wells (2009)

Figure 1.3 Evolution of the main CBT therapies.

to address particular problems, for example in Dialectical Behavior Therapy (DBT) (Linehan, 1993) and Schema Focussed Therapy (SFT) (Young, 1994) the focus is on the treatment of personality disorders. In Mindfulness Based Cognitive Therapy (MBT) (Segal *et al.*, 2002) the focus has been on relapse prevention in depression, and in Problem Solving Therapy (PST) (Nezu and Nezu, 1989) the target disorder was also depression. In both Acceptance and Commitment Therapy (ACT) (Hayes *et al.*, 1999) and Rational Emotive Therapy (RET) (Ellis, 1962) the approaches are transdiagnostic. Older CBT therapies are sometimes adapted for other purposes, for example Meichenbaum's SIT (1985) includes self-instruction training, in which a client is taught coping self-statements for use (a) in advance of a stressor, (b) when encountering the stressor, (c) when feeling overwhelmed by the stressor and (d) when reflecting on the management of the stressor. Scott (2012) has utilised self-instruction training to distil a non-trauma focussed CBT intervention for post-traumatic stress disorder. In a similar manner Nezu, Nezu and Lombardo (2004) have refined PST (Nezu and Nezu, 1989) so that problem solving acts as a substrate for disorder specific CBT interventions for depression, the anxiety disorders, borderline personality disorder, male erectile disorder, couple distress and anger problems.

There have been few direct comparisons of the different CBTs and those that have been made have yet to demonstrate an added value over earlier CBTs. For example, Arch *et al.* (2012) compared traditional CBT with ACT in a sample of mixed anxiety disorders and found that both treatments were equally effective. These authors found that the response rate of approximately 50 per cent was comparable to the average mean response rate for CBT across anxiety disorder studies from 2000–2011. However in both CBT and ACT in the Arch *et al.* (2012) study, approximately one in three clients dropped out. Approximately four out of five clients in the Arch *et al.* (2012) study suffered from either panic disorder, generalised anxiety disorder or social phobia. Whilst clients with OCD and specific phobias were included in the study, there were so few (nine OCD sufferers in the CBT arm and eight OCD sufferers in the ACT arm, two clients with a specific phobia in the CBT arm and four clients with a specific phobia in the ACT arm) that the relevance of the study to these disorders is questionable; further, clients with PTSD were not included in the analyses. Early on in treatment CBT was rated as a more credible treatment than ACT. There are difficulties with the external validity of the Arch *et al.* (2012) study, in that clients had on average three and a half years of college education, were fee paying and recruited by the media and by referral. These authors expressed the hope that some CBTs may be found more useful for some clients than others. Clearly, if this were the case response rates could be increased but there is little evidence of this to date.

The evidence base for each CBT has to be assessed on its merits, as it cannot be assumed that each of the CBTs is as potent as the others and that each could be regarded as an empirically supported treatment as defined by Chambless and Hollon (1998), see Appendix C.

The structure of CBT supervision

Supervision sessions are traditionally modelled on the standard structure of CBT sessions. The Beck Institute website (www.beckinstitute.org) gives the following capsule summary of the format of a supervision session:

> conduct a brief check-in, collaboratively set the agenda, establish a 'bridge' from the previous supervision session to the current one, discuss the case (including conceptualization, direct teaching, guided discovery, and role-playing), discuss other topics or patients (if time allows), help participants create an 'action plan' to follow up the supervision session, and elicit feedback from the participant.

The Beck Institute provides weekly hour-long supervision sessions and this is also the recommendation of *Improving Access to Psychological Therapies* (Turpin and Wheeler, 2011). However the BABCP (British Association of Behavioural and Cognitive Psychotherapies) recommendation is for a minimum of one hour a month (Lewis, 2012). Further supervision is time limited at the Beck Institute (23 or 46 weeks) whereas for UK CBT therapists it is open-ended. When group supervision is the mode of supervision, this typically involves up to four supervisees and the recommendation is that group sessions should be one and a half to two hours long.

Figure 1.2 indicates that the supervisor is reliant on the accuracy of the supervisees' account of their transactions with the client in forming a judgement as to the appropriateness of treatment strategies employed. But a study of psychiatry students suggests that reports of a clinical interview contain significant inaccuracies when compared to a videotape of the interview, with over half (54 per cent) of the themes of the latter unreported (Muslin, Thumblad and Meschel, 1981). Such considerations have led to the videoing of supervisees' CBT treatment sessions (indeed it is now mandatory within BABCP – Lewis, 2012) and their examination by a supervisor. In order to assess a supervisee's competence supervisors have usually used the Cognitive Therapy Rating Scale (Young and Beck, 1980). Group supervision involving up to four participants is sometimes used in lieu of individual supervision and similarly involves use of recordings.

In the UK the background of CBT therapists undergoing supervision is extremely varied, with no set academic background or clinical experience. By contrast at the Beck Institute supervisees are expected to hold at least Masters degrees and to ordinarily have completed a three-day introductory workshop.

Does CBT supervision deliver?

Supervisees appear generally content with supervision – positive effects of supervision on supervisees include enhanced self-awareness, enhanced treatment knowledge, skill acquisition and utilisation, enhanced self-efficacy and strengthening of the supervisee–patient relationship (Watkins, 2011). In a study of 160 UK cognitive behavioural practitioners, Townend, Iannetta and Freeston (2002) found only one person was very dissatisfied with supervision, 33 per cent reported being 'very satisfied', 44 per cent 'satisfied', 9 per cent 'undecided' and 8 per cent 'dissatisfied'. However the evidence that CBT supervision positively affects client outcomes is slender:

1   Bambling *et al.* (2006) compared the effects of the provision of supervision and no supervision amongst therapists providing problem solving therapy (PST) for depression. (PST is an established CBT for depression involving the following stages: problem orientation, problem definition, brainstorming of solutions, choice of solution, experimentation with the chosen solution and return to the menu of options if the identified problem is not resolved or only partially resolved (Nezu and Perri, 1989).) The clients of therapists undergoing supervision did significantly better than the clients of therapists not undergoing supervision. Further, the proportion of clients of non-supervised therapists not completing the eight-session programme was 35 per cent, by comparison with only 4.5 per cent of the clients of supervised therapists failing to complete the eight-session programme. In this study, supervision focussed on the therapeutic alliance, involving a three pronged focus: bond, task and goal. The supervisors were concerned to ensure that therapist and clients were in agreement with regard to tasks and goals and that a relationship was developed between therapist and client. Further the supervisors followed a manual for the fostering of a therapeutic alliance.

2   Bradshaw *et al.* (2007) trained supervisors, via a two-day course, to supervise nurses delivering a family and cognitive-behavioural intervention to the care givers of patients with schizophrenia. The results were compared to the same interventions delivered to another group of care givers without any supervision provided. Those patients who were indirectly linked to supervision showed a greater reduction in hallucinations and delusional beliefs and in total psychotic symptoms.

3   White and Winstanley (2010) trained supervisors via a four-day course, and supervised nurses over the course of a year; the results were compared with patient outcomes where there was no supervision provided. However no significant differences emerged between patients indirectly linked to a supervisor and those who were not. The diagnostic status of clients was not assessed using a standardised diagnostic interview and there was no indication that the nurses involved used a cognitive behavioural programme.

Commentary: The above studies suggest that CBT supervision is probably efficacious. But they leave largely unanswered whether CBT supervision in routine practice is effective. CBT supervision in routine practice rarely has the therapeutic alliance as its main focus, as in the Bambling *et al.* (2006) study and with probable good reason, as studies have shown that the therapeutic alliance predicts no more than 6 per cent of variance in outcome (Safran and Muran, 2006). Further, in routine practice the diagnostic status of a client is rarely established using a standardised structured interview as in the Bambling *et al.* (2006) study and the focus of supervisees is on clients with a wide range of disorders/difficulties. In the Bambling *et al.* (2006) study although those clients linked indirectly to supervision did, statistically, significantly better than those depressed clients not linked to supervision, the initial Beck depression scores of 'supervised' and 'unsupervised' clients was 30, the end of treatment score of the latter was 12 and the former 7. A question can therefore be raised about whether supervision was cost-effective given the small difference between end-of-treatment scores. Nevertheless therapists who were supervised were significantly more able to engage clients for the duration of the treatment programme. In both the Bambling *et al.* study (2006) and the Bradshaw *et al.* study (2007) the focus was on the treatment of a specific population (clients with depression and psychosis respectively). Thus, although there may be gains to supervision in these tightly defined contexts, it is unknown whether this will generalise to routine practice. The White and Winstanley (2010) study suggests that the supervision of therapists delivering a generic counselling does not produce measurable gains in patient outcomes. The Bradshaw *et al.* study (2007) and the White and Winstanley study (2010) also raise the question of whether satisfactory attendance at a two- or four-day workshop should qualify a person to be a supervisor.

The important question may be not *whether* CBT supervision can deliver but *what type* of CBT supervision works, with which supervisees, in which circumstances? Supervisees may vary along many dimensions, e.g. low intensity IAPT workers vs. high intensity IAPT workers (IAPT, 2008), experienced vs. inexperienced. The contexts in which supervisees operate may also vary along many dimensions, e.g. adult vs. child and adolescent mental health, serious mental illness vs. depression and anxiety disorders. At present there is little by way of an answer to this question, but the Bambling *et al.* (2006) study may have pointed the way forward for supervision research by detailing a manual for use by supervisors and the specification of a target disorder.

Supervision, in general is often justified because of its effects on staff retention and the prevention of burnout (e.g. Wallbank and Hatton, 2011) and there is evidence that in social work and social care good supervision is associated with job satisfaction, commitment to the organisation and retention (Carpenter, Webb, Bostock and Coomber, 2012). But Carpenter and colleagues (2012) also conclude that 'overall, the empirical basis for supervision in social work and social care in the UK is weak. Most of the evidence is correlational and derives from child welfare services in the US.' It would be surprising if CBT supervision did not also prove to have a positive effect on job satisfaction/burnout, commitment to the organisation and retention, but this remains to be demonstrated. Further, as in social work, the evidence base for the effects of CBT supervision on client outcomes is, to date, slender.

In search of a credible CBT supervisor

The supervisor needs to be upfront from the outset about the limits of their own knowledge of CBT and whether they can tailor this knowledge sufficiently to be of use to the supervisee. For example a supervisor may be well versed in the CBT treatment of adult depression and anxiety disorders but if the supervisee's practice context is child and adolescent mental health, the supervisor needs to be alert as to how possible gaps in his/her knowledge base could be resolved.

The relationship between supervisor and supervisee can be complicated if the supervisor has a dual relationship with the supervisee, e.g. line manager and supervisor or sometimes friend/partner and supervisor. Townend, Ianetta and Freeston (2002) found 38 per cent of their sample of UK cognitive behaviour therapists were in dual relationships. However, comparatively few of those with dual relationships (17.5 per cent) said that this had created difficulties in supervision.

The CBT supervisor as a conduit for Evidence Based Treatment

Supervision has been an integral part of randomised controlled trials (RCTs) of disorder specific CBT protocols for emotional disorders. One of the functions of supervision in RCTs has been to ensure treatment integrity, i.e. that the therapist is conducting treatment according to the specified manual for the targeted disorder. Butler *et al.* (2006) conducted a meta-analysis of RCTs of CBT and found large effect sizes for depression, generalised anxiety disorder, panic disorder (with or without agoraphobia), social phobia, posttraumatic stress disorder (PTSD) and childhood depressive and anxiety disorders. Marital distress, anger, childhood somatic disorders and chronic pain showed moderate effect sizes. More recently, Hofman and Smits (2008) have replicated these findings across the adult anxiety disorders. Thus CBT supervision takes place against a background of evidence based treatments (EBTs) and these are, or should be, the currency of CBT supervision sessions. The supervisor may play a pivotal role in helping the supervisee translate findings from the research setting to routine practice: for example, a client with PTSD may also have mild learning difficulties, necessitating some adaptation to the standard protocol. But CBT supervision also requires the monitoring of adherence to evidence-based CBT interventions and ensuring the measurement of client outcomes. In this volume the importance of the framework of Table 1.1 is taken as read, and the emphasis is on the distinguishing aspects of CBT – rather in the way basic counselling skills of empathy, warmth, genuineness, etc. are taken as an intrinsic part of a therapist's modus operandi and CBT courses therefore emphasise the acquisition of a technical competence to complement the fundamentals. Table 1.1 is most applicable to individual supervision; there are additional considerations for the supervisee who is involved in group supervision, such as inclusion, and these are discussed in Chapter 9.

The supervisee as engineer

The scientist-practitioner model can be traced back to the Boulder Conference in 1949 on Graduate Education in Clinical Psychology (Benjamin and Baker, 2000) and the same model has been adopted for the training/practice of CBT therapists. The scientist-practitioner model is summarised in Figure 1.4.

Aaron T. Beck, the founder of cognitive therapy, is an exemplar of the scientist-practitioner model embodied in Figure 1.4. In the 1950s he decided to test out the psychoanalytic theory that depression is anger turned inward (hypothesis – 11 o'clock position) by asking depressed patients in a private practice sample about the content of their dreams (testing out of hypothesis – the 1 o'clock position). In fact, his hypothesis was not supported. The content of dreams in depressed patients was similar to the content of their waking thoughts (self-critical, pessimistic, and negative). The results were published (the 6 o'clock position in Figure 1.4) at the end of the decade by Beck and Hurvich (1959), and this was the precursor to developing, in the following decade, a new empirically based theory of depression and a new psychotherapy, cognitive therapy (the 8 o'clock position in Figure 1.4). In turn, further hypotheses (back to the 11 o'clock position) have been tested, such as the cognitive content specificity hypothesis that disorders are distinguished by their cognitive content (Alford and Beck, 1997). The above model of the Scientist-Practitioner in Operation is consistent with Kolb's (1984) Learning Cycle, and supervision as an experiential learning activity. Going clockwise around Figure 1.4, a hypothesis is tested and the results constitute a concrete experience which is reflected upon and set in a wider context. The re-formulation

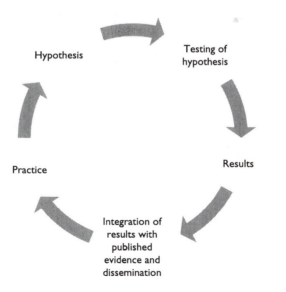

Figure 1.4 The scientist-practitioner in operation.

is then put into practice and a further hypothesis is generated. Although the scientist-practitioner model has borne a great deal of fruit, the proportion of CBT practitioners who have the resources to conduct experiments and have the results published is small indeed, confined largely to academic clinicians who are primarily funded by a university. The academic clinicians are scientists characterised by a search for specific answers to their own research and writing. Most CBT practitioners are front-line clinicians, and their concerns are technical/engineering: (a) how to perform particular tasks, (b) how to solve particular problems, (c) how to learn about new approaches relevant to their particular tasks and (d) how to acquire and expand background knowledge helpful to the performance of their tasks.

In terms of Figure 1.4 the scientist-practitioner model breaks down for the vast majority of CBT practitioners at the 1 o'clock and 6 o'clock positions. It may be that a better working model for the majority of CBT practitioners is that of an engineer. Engineers make an advanced synthesis of pure maths, physics, chemistry, etc., in the same way a practitioner might test out the acceptability of prolonged exposure for PTSD in routine practice (Scott and Stradling, 1997) or whether group cognitive therapy is viable in a deprived inner city area (Scott and Stradling, 1990); thus the practitioner's focus is on the application of what has been demonstrated to be efficacious. However, although an engineering model may be a better descriptor of the practice of most CBT practitioners as they try to adapt findings from research trials to their setting, there are still major problems of time and resources in the distillation and publication of results.

Shapiro (2002) has observed that 'well-established treatments can be cost-effectively delivered by expert therapists, who need not be scientist-practitioners', and this casts further doubts on whether the scientist-practitioner model should be normative for CBT practitioners. Arguably, given that the greatest challenge facing CBT is one of dissemination (Shafran *et al.*, 2009), there should be more emphasis on the engineering and less on the scientist-practitioner. Supervision would then be reconstructed as largely facilitating 'engineering' rather than the development of scientist-practitioners.

Beck *et al.* (1979) recommended that the relationship between therapist and client should be one of 'collaborative empiricism', i.e. that there is a relationship of equality between therapist and client and they jointly discover the appropriate ways forward. As such, the therapist should eschew didactic instruction in sessions in favour of guided discovery. But collaboration and empiricism are at least as much a part of an engineer's working as a scientist's: engineers may for example collaborate with medics on the most appropriate material for a heart valve or hip replacement and will evaluate the consequences of the chosen materials. The engineer brings a scientific interpretation and perception to their endeavours as much as a scientist and it is the transmission of this framework to the client that is a goal of 'collaborative empiricism' (Overholser, 2011).

Pick and mix

The jury is largely out on whether the newer CBTs represent a 'forward leap' or 'backward somersault'. The danger is that therapists confronted with such a plethora of CBTs 'pick and mix' from the differing CBT therapies. In such instances the supervisor will need to make the supervisee aware that such an admixture is neither evidence based nor theoretically consistent. But this presupposes that the supervisor knows the similarities and differences between the therapies and which of them are known to work for what, under what circumstances. Without this guidance the supervisee may be like a young child let loose in a supermarket, possibly making themselves ill and not assisting shoppers (clients).

Kazdin (2008) defined evidence based treatments (EBTs) as interventions or techniques that have 'produced therapeutic change in controlled trials' (p. 147), and evidence-based practice (EBP) as a broader term referring to 'clinical practice that is informed by evidence about interventions, clinical expertise, and patient needs, values, and preferences, and their integration in decision-making about individual care' (p. 147). This raises the question of whether the role of the supervisor is to promote EBT or EBP or both and to what extent? Adverts for CBT workshops rarely contain information about particular empirically supported interventions nor do they cite scientific evidence for the effectiveness of the treatments advertised. Anecdotally, today June 13th 2012, the author's e-mails contained invites to three different workshops 'A Brief Introduction to Compassion Focussed Therapy', 'Transdiagnostic CBT Using the Method of Levels' and 'CBT for Clinical Perfectionism across Presentations'. These probably would not be regarded as EBTs (as defined by Chambless and Hollon (1998), see Appendix C) but doubtless the authors of the workshops would argue that they are EBPs. However, the definition of an EBP ('clinical practice that is informed by evidence about interventions . . .') is worryingly vague, so that almost any intervention could be subsumed under it. As Kazdin (2011) has pointed out there has been almost no research on EBPs compared to EBTs (the terms EBTs and Evidence Supported Treatments (ESTs) are used interchangeably in this volume). Whilst there are some slight differences in the criteria for EBTs, they have in common that they have been subjected to a randomised clinical trial and have been found more effective than a comparison condition (waiting list control or an active treatment condition), further, the results have been replicated by a group independent of those conducting the initial positive trial. Evidence-based practice has not been studied and raises (Kazdin, 2011) multiple issues about, for example, the vagaries of decision making, and no guiding rules for decision making if all treatment is individually tailored.

EBTs have for the most part been diagnosis specific, i.e. different protocols for different disorders. It therefore follows that it is not possible to provide EBTs without first an accurate diagnosis. However there are those who see diagnosis as anathema and Kinderman *et al.* (2013) write:

the most useful approach would be to develop individual formulations, consisting of a summary of an individual's problems and circumstances, hypothesis about their origins and possible therapeutic solutions. This 'problem definition, formulation' approach rather than a 'diagnosis treatment' approach would yield all the benefits of the current approach without its many inadequacies and dangers, the trouble is that this has not been proved and until such time as it is there is a case for EBTs.

With regard to EBPs the supervisor faces a particular challenge: on the one hand there is a need to be open to new developments that *may* offer added value to established EBTs; on the other hand there is a need to retain a critical stance as to whether evidence of effectiveness has been demonstrated (see Chapter Two of Roth and Fonagy's (2005) seminal work, 'What Works for Whom?' for an excellent discussion of what constitutes evidence). One of the roles of the supervisor is to make a supervisee aware of the distinction between an EBT and an EBP and the nuances of each. Without such an appreciation the supervisee may 'pick and mix' extensively and inappropriately.

Chapter 2

Supervision and clinical decision making

Beyond the certainties of birth and death, there is also the certainty that the therapist will get 'stuck' at some point in treating a client. Such stumbling blocks often become a focus in supervision. The supervisor can usefully translate the supervisee's concern into a question 'what intervention, would be appropriate with this client, in these circumstances?' In this way the concerns of the supervisee are located in the domain of evidence based treatments (EBTs). The supervisor may or may not feel they have the answer to the question posed, nevertheless they should be engaged in a collaborative endeavour with the supervisee and if necessary pertinent other 'experts', in discovering a solution that the client may judge as viable. But distilling the appropriate treatment pathway can be marred by cognitive errors and the focus of this chapter is on helping the supervisor side step these information processing biases.

Just as a client's behaviours may be governed by cognitive processing errors, neither the therapist, supervisor nor another 'expert' are immune from such errors. For example a supervisee may not take difficulties with a particular client to supervision because they believe 'I ought to show my supervisor how good I am'. Equally the supervisor might berate themselves along the lines of 'I ought to know the answer to the supervisee's question without having to sound out a colleague'. Similarly a consulted 'expert' might give an opinion on treatment but may be working on a silent assumption such as 'Attention Deficit Hyperactivity Disorder wreaks havoc, many prison inmates start their criminal trajectory with it, better to treat this child as if ADHD'. Thus the, Cognitive Dispositions to Respond (CDRs) (Makhinson, 2012) can have a major influence on decision making. The notion of CDRs draws on the early work of Kahneman, Slovic and Tversky (1982), who described the way in which rules of thumb (heuristics) are often employed when individuals are presented with complex information under conditions of uncertainty, bypassing detailed analysis. More recently, Kahneman (2011) has extended the library of heuristics to include the affect heuristic, this reflects how judgement can be affected by momentary changes in mood. For example a fresh light breeze blowing through the window on a sultry day, might affect whether a supervisor challenges a supervisee over not giving notice of non-attendance at the previous supervision session. When focussed on a 'stumbling

Table 2.1 Moving on in supervision

Supervisee's perception of stumbling block	Supervisor's first thoughts	What CDRs might be operating?	Gameplan

block' in treatment both the supervisor and supervisee need to appraise their first thoughts by passing them through a CDR filter in order to arrive at a game plan, Table 2.1.

Table 2.1 is a framework for helping supervisees move on from 'stuck points' in treatment. It is also a reminder that the supervisor's first thoughts can be subject to biases as much as the supervisee's and that both may need circumventing to distil a game plan.

Cognitive Dispositions to Respond (CDRs)

CDRs are information processing biases that can short circuit the delivery of evidence-based treatment. Supervision acts as a 'firewall' to CDRs. The CDRs in Table 2.2 are not intended to be exhaustive and there is some overlap between them.

The following dialogue illustrates the identification of CDRs in a supervision session:

SUPERVISEE: I don't think Maria wants to get better, she is the baby of the family and everyone fusses over her. She went to the Pain Management Group but she is still complaining about pain.

SUPERVISOR: What makes you think that she doesn't want to get better?

SUPERVISEE: She still just travels in a car when she has to, like to an appointment, I've explained to her that if she wants to get over the problem she needs to dare herself to travel by car as often as before.

SUPERVISOR: What are Maria's problems?

SUPERVISEE: PTSD.

SUPERVISOR: What proportion of clients respond to CBT for PTSD?

Table 2.2 Common CDRs

1. Availability heuristic	Assuming that something is highly probable because it is very vivid, e.g. the everyday nature of the last encounter with a client before they commited suicide.
2. Representative heuristic	Using one instance of a category as a template for assessing whether others are part of the same category, e.g. no horrific nightmares like X's PTSD, so this client does not have real PTSD.
3. Confirmatory bias	Once a conclusion is arrived at, seeking only information that confirms the conclusion, e.g. administering a psychometric test for the identified problem, without conducting a broad screen.
4. Affect heuristic	Being unduly influenced by the mood of the moment, e.g. discharging a client from treatment because of their recent improvement but without any evidence that they have acquired coping skills.
5. Anchoring bias	Focussing early on in treatment on an unusual feature of the client's presentation and construing further information in the light of this, e.g. that the client was a clergyman.
6. Aggregate bias	The belief that one's clients are somehow exceptional, not like those in research studies, e.g. if there are difficulties with a client, it must be a 'complex' case.
7. Diagnostic momentum	Once diagnostic labels are applied to a client they become stickier and stickier, e.g. a client seen by mental health services for ten years with depression was never asked whether they were abused in childhood nor enquiry made about possible PTSD symptoms
8. Premature decision making	Stopping at the first conclusion, failing to enquire about other possibilities, e.g. it is concluded that an elderly lady is depressed but she has not been asked about her alcohol consumption.
9. Fundamental attribution error	The tendency to blame the client for lack of therapeutic improvement, e.g. lack of motivation or secondary gain.
10. Base-rate neglect	The tendency to ignore base rates, e.g. knowing ADHD is commoner in boys than girls, but 'identifying' it 9 times as often in caseload as opposed to the 3 times as often that research shows.

SUPERVISEE: I don't know, most?
SUPERVISOR: It is 40–70 per cent.
SUPERVISEE: So it might not be that she does not want to get better?
SUPERVISOR: Could be?

In this exchange, the supervisor has identified two CDRs that the supervisee has been using: Base-rate Neglect, and Fundamental Attribution Error. The dialogue continues:

SUPERVISOR: You seem to have been using some information processing biases, (9 and 10 in Table 2.2), you might want to look at them and other biases that clinicians sometimes use. Once you become aware of them you can more easily step around them.

SUPERVISEE: It's a bit like alerting a client to mental filters, all or nothing thinking and all the other information processing biases from the Burns (1999) book.

SUPERVISOR: Yes biases, are not unique to clients, my wife says I have one, if something goes wrong it is her or somebody else's fault and if they go well it is because of me.

SUPERVISEE: You may need some serious treatment!

SUPERVISOR: Motivational deficits I'm afraid!

The above exchange is intended to convey that biases are the human lot and that the supervisee is not to be 'pathologised' for discovering that he/she has operated on them.

CDRs and assessment

Supervisors are advised by BABCP (see BABCP supervisor's report www.babcp. com) to assess supervisees by regularly reviewing audio or DVDs of sessions. The practice is for supervisees periodically to provide a recording of a session which is listened to/watched by the supervisor. But any one treatment session is necessarily a cross-section of what has happened at one point in treatment, the material has no context. It is not known, for example, whether the focus in a session is on anything that was an identified treatment target at the start, i.e. whether key cognitions and behaviours are being targeted. For example the treatment strategy being demonstrated might be the mechanics of a relaxation exercise which may be well taught, the client's understanding ascertained but there is no empirical evidence that this strategy is pertinent to a client's depression identified in the first interview. Unwittingly in viewing one session the supervisor will be looking for instances of confirmation of what the supervisee suggests in the session, e.g. if the supervisee suggests anger management is an important issue the supervisor will look for instances where the client expresses they have an anger problem and may discount disconfirming utterances from the client, e.g. 'sometimes I think he is doing it deliberately' and evidence is not sought from the initial assessment interview that might disconfirm that the client has an anger problem. The single session assessment is particularly open to confirmatory bias. If a supervisor has had the opportunity to listen to a First Interview, not only can they rate the quality of the assessment but there then become a limited range of appropriate treatment strategies and it is much easier to gauge, at a subsequent session, whether the supervisee has stepped outside the range.

Again when viewing one session the supervisor may be more subject to the affect heuristic, e.g. a client may be saying that the CBT is not working, the supervisor catches the low mood and has a more jaundiced view of the supervisee's conduct of the session. Had the supervisor been privy to an initial assessment they may have been alerted that this client had not only axis 1 disorders but also personality disorders.

First interviews are rarely assessed by supervisors, but without these anchors, assessment of subsequents sessions may be flawed.

Heuristics and power differentials

There is a power differential between supervisor and supervisee just as there is between therapist and client. In both cases there is a danger that the least powerful member of the dyad engages in an activity, e.g. a particular homework assignment, not because of the credibility of the argument put forward, but because of the status of the most powerful member of the dyad. In terms of the Elaboration Likelihood Model of Persuasion (Petty and Cacioppo, 1986) the least powerful member of a dyad may use peripheral processing, e.g. 'if he/she says so it must be right', rather than central (effortful processing requiring attention) processing and engagement in the behaviour, e.g. homework, might not be long lasting. Central processing depends not only on the motivation of the recipient of a message but also on ability. It is therefore crucial that the supervisor/therapist very carefully checks out the message they have conveyed has been understood and that it is supported by an evidence base, the following exchange re: a client with Obsessive Compulsive Disorder in relation to contamination fears illustrates this:

SUPERVISOR: You should get your client to wipe his hand around the bowl of the loo and lick it, to show there is no danger of contamination.
SUPERVISEE: I can't get him to use a public loo.
SUPERVISOR: You could demonstrate it using the loo in work.
SUPERVISEE: How do you know that works?
SUPERVISOR: It is exposure and response prevention!
SUPERVISEE: I have not read that strategy in any of the OCD outcome studies.
SUPERVISOR: Now I come to think of it neither have I, I will look into it.

In this exchange the supervisee has resisted pursuing an eminence-based intervention and has stood his/her ground insisting that intervention be evidence-based and the supervisor in fairness has halted and in a spirit of collaborative empiricism has agreed to pursue matters further. The next supervision session continued:

SUPERVISOR: After our last session I looked up the trials and you were right. The strategy I mentioned doesn't feature in them, it comes from the 'elegant' solution in Rational Emotive Therapy.
SUPERVISEE: I thought it would be too big a jump for a client who will not even go into a public loo.

SUPERVISOR: I was also reading about the Elaboration Likelihood Model of Persuasion in Social Psychology (Petty and Cacioppo, 1986), and they make the point that people are more likely to take on board a new argument if it is close to their existing attitude. On reflection, what I was suggesting is far away from what most members of the public would do and light years from where your client is, so it probably wasn't a very bright idea.

This exchange highlights that certain intervention strategies may be very dramatic, vivid, easily recalled and a supervisor is as likely to recommend them (availability heuristic) as much as supervisee, instead of pausing to see if they are justified. The errors in processing are likely to continue if the supervisee is engaged in peripheral processing.

The operation of heuristics in power differentials can be quite subtle, particularly where children are clients, as the following dialogue illustrates:

SUPERVISOR: How is it going with the ten-year-old who was run over a couple of years ago?

SUPERVISEE: I asked Jasmin to draw a ladder of 'dares' that she might gradually climb up, start doing some 'dares' and having a special time for writing about what upset her.

SUPERVISOR: Did she do the homeworks?

SUPERVISEE: She said she had done just one dare, went to the toilet upstairs by herself. Brought in her writing but forgot to bring in the ladder which she said wasn't complete. Jasmin also completed this Child Post-traumatic Stress Cognitions Inventory (Meiser-Stedman *et al.*, 2009), *handing it to the supervisor.*

SUPERVISOR: Looking at her responses she clearly sees the world as a scary place but she also thinks she is crazy and permanently damaged. What is your game plan (Table 2.2) for addressing 'crazy, permanently damaged'?

SUPERVISEE: I thought I would keep it simple, just concentrating on her behaviours.

SUPERVISOR: But does she understand why she should do the 'dares'?

SUPERVISEE: I explained to her that getting your confidence in the world is like getting your confidence in water, you have to gradually get in the water.

SUPERVISOR: That's a great metaphor something a child could easily grasp, but what about her fear that she is 'crazy, permanently damaged'.

SUPERVISEE: I guess I'm hoping those ideas will clear up as she goes out more by herself.

SUPERVISOR: They could if she does do the 'dares', but she doesn't seem too hot on the 'dares' at present, I appreciate that you have tried to put her in control by having her construct the ladder, but there are shades of 'do "dares" because I say so'. If you were explaining to an adult, why they should attempt 'dares', what would you say?

SUPERVISEE: I would probably tell them about having developed a hypersensitive alarm as a consequence of their accident and the need to reset the alarm.

SUPERVISOR: What would stop you translating that information for consumption by Jasmin? Perhaps describing that she has got a 'faulty alarm' might help her feel less 'crazy', and as 'dares' are about resetting the alarm, she may be more likely to engage in them.

SUPERVISEE: I suppose I'm using a heuristic, 'with kids keep it simple, concentrate on behaviour'.

SUPERVISOR: And the evidence is?

This exchange illustrates how a supervisee with a child client can unwittingly slip into a parent–child interaction rather than become collaboratively involved in the child's treatment. In this dialogue supervisor and supervisee have implicitly used the framework of Table 2.1. In terms of the first column in Table 2.1, the supervisee did not perceive that there was a stumbling block in the child's engagement of behavioural experiments but the supervisor thought, second column of Table 2.1, there was some evidence of non-compliance and in the third column it would have been appropriate with the supervisee's agreement, to write the supervisee's CDR, 'just focus on behaviour with kids'. In the final column of Table 2.1 the supervisor has suggested a game plan to facilitate the required behaviour change with an age appropriate cognitive intervention.

Heuristics and randomised controlled trials

CDRs may affect whether RCTs are used as a benchmark for treatment. For example, if each individual is seen as unique and pride of place is given to unfettered clinical judgement (the Aggregate Bias in Table 2.1) then RCTs become simply a market place in which a variety of treatment techniques and approaches are on display, that they are, for the most part, diagnosis specific protocols is not centrally processed. Randomised controlled trials are at the top of the hierarchy of the evidence to be considered for treatment. However, RCTs may not be without biases themselves. An invitation bias may operate when, typically GPs, are invited to refer patients with a particular disorder to a prestigious research centre and may hold back the most disturbed of their patients with regard to the disorder in question. A volunteer bias may operate in studies where subjects are recruited via advertisements, i.e. those responding to an advertisement may be different to the general clinical population. An allegiance bias may operate in cases where committed CBT therapists are comparing the efficacy of a CBT intervention but are also involved in delivering a comparison condition such as supportive counselling. A possible lack of commitment to the latter may make the results questionable.

Chapter 3

Matching supervisor and supervisee

A supervisor needs not only experience of the practice of CBT, but also an appreciation of the problems surrounding the application of that knowledge in the context in which the supervisee is working. The supervisor is required to be cognisant of research but an engineer, in the sense of the adaptation of that knowledge to the particular circumstances of the supervisee. Whilst there may occasionally be an advantage in supervisor and supervisee having worked in largely different areas, in that strategies utilised in one context can be candidates for consideration of application in the other, generally there are likely to be some difficulties. However, in practice perfect matches between supervisor and supervisee are often not available, so 'good enough' matches suffice and may be the most enriching, provided the potential pitfalls are made explicit. A supervisor cannot assume, because a supervisee requests CBT supervision, that the latter has the same allegiance to it and this may make for difficulties. Just as the treatment of a client has to be culturally sensitive so too does supervision, and in this chapter the focus is on ensuring that the supervisor and supervisee are 'singing from the same hymn sheet'.

Not knowing what you do not know

A supervisor may in good faith agree a contract with a supervisee, but be unaware of deficits in their knowledge in the domain in which the latter is operating. For example a supervisor may have worked entirely in Adult Mental Health but their supervisee may be working in Child and Adolescent Mental Health, and may not keep as abreast of the literature in the latter domain. In such circumstances the supervisor may easily fall prey to the heuristics (CDRs) detailed in Chapter Two. The supervisor may draw upon his/her experiences of conducting generic CBT with adults, utilising an availability heuristic, and see these as a template (representativeness heuristic) of what to recommend to his supervisee working in CAMHS. However a recent meta-analysis conducted by Reynolds, Wilson, Austin and Hooper (2012) has shown treatment targeted at specific anxiety disorders had larger effects than treatment targeted at a range of anxiety disorders.

Knowing the terrain of the supervisee

Supervisees working outside of mainline NHS and high intensity IAPT may face particular problems in finding a suitable supervisor. Probably most supervisors have little or no experience of providing a low intensity IAPT service, running a private practice or of providing CBT as part of an in-house Occupational Health Service or as an external provider to such a Service. In such circumstances the chance of a mismatch between supervisor and supervisee increases. The danger is that the supervisor will minimise the significance of these difficulties by use of the representative heuristic, assuming that what the supervisee faces in these contexts will largely mirror his/her own experience.

CBT in occupational health

The following example illustrates how the standard training of a CBT therapist may leave a supervisor feeling inadequate, when confronted with a supervisee working in an Occupational Health context:

SUPERVISEE: My client John is depressed, since he fell down the steps at work injuring his left hand. The Specialist has said he is effectively permanently now just one handed, has localised chronic regional pain syndrome and he has been off work since.

SUPERVISOR: How active is he keeping himself at home?

SUPERVISEE: Oh his mood improves when he does a bit of voluntary work with people with mild learning difficulties but then it goes down, he worries about work and the financial pressures on his family.

SUPERVISOR: Maybe you could do the worry time strategy over work and the financial pressures.

SUPERVISEE: Tried that, but he is still fed up over work and his finances.

SUPERVISOR: What is it about work that he is fed up with?

SUPERVISEE: Management want him back and say they will make arrangements for him and have suggested he might mind the machines for the men when they are on their lunch, but he has said the men will be annoyed if he has to call them back because something has gone wrong. He will feel like a spare part.

SUPERVISOR: Maybe you could work on his low self-esteem.

SUPERVISEE: John thinks they only want him back so they don't have to pay out as much in compensation, then when there are further redundancies in 12 months or so they will get rid of him.

SUPERVISOR: Is he being paranoid?

SUPERVISEE: I wouldn't put it past them, but what can I say? Providing CBT is a way of management being seen to have done the right thing.

Unless the supervisor has also had Occupational Psychology training he/she is likely to be unaware that the Organisational Climate can be an important factor in an employee's stress. Further lack of role clarity is also a well-known stressor – the supervisee could suggest to the employer that a newly written job description might lessen anxiety but that in order to do this the capability of the client needed to be assessed. The supervisee might also raise with the employer the likelihood of the client being able to persist with a task, complete it in a timely manner and handle the everyday hassles of the workplace.

CBT in private practice

The following examples taken from private practice also illustrate how the traditional CBT training of a supervisor may be inadequate to the task facing a supervisee:

SUPERVISEE: I was fed up when Brian, the young gambler, didn't turn up again. His parents contacted me and paid for him to attend the first two sessions and he agreed to see how six sessions would work out.

SUPERVISOR: How motivated is he?

SUPERVISEE: I used the Motivation ruler (Scott, 2011), which suggested he was in the contemplation rather than the action stage with regard to giving up his gambling.

SUPERVISOR: Maybe it is not too surprising he did not turn up.

SUPERVISEE: But I've got bills to pay, I even had to go to a Food Resource Centre for my son and I, I was relying on those sessions. The company I get referrals from want me to provide just six sessions and a report at the end; they take me hours. I can't afford to say 'no' but how do you provide CBT in six sessions!

SUPERVISOR: Pass.

In the above example the supervisor's training is of limited value in assisting the supervisee, but if the supervisor had had experience of private practice, the issue of marketing would have been uppermost in his/her mind. The supervisor may have suggested that the supervisee set themselves up as a Company marketing his/her wares to the new GP Commisioning Groups. Further using a marketing frame-work, the supervisor may have suggested to the supervisee that he/she first of all clarifies what the customers (GPs/Organisations) want before selling her 'product'.

CBT in low intensity IAPT

A supervisee working in a low intensity IAPT programme is working in a context that is likely to be very different to that which the great majority of supervisors have experienced. In low intensity IAPT (Richards and Borglin, 2011) clients have an initial face-to-face contact with a case manager following which clients are offered telephone contacts for subsequent appointments although face-to-face appointments could be available. A supervisor is involved with the case manager and client in deciding whether the client should be stepped up to a higher intensity treatment. Low intensity treatment focussed on self-help manuals for depression (Lovell and

Richards, 2007) and anxiety (Williams, 2003). Two computerised programmes 'Beating the Blues' and 'Fear Fighter' were also offered to clients. The mean number of sessions was 5.5 over 3.5 hours; however, only 53 per cent of clients received two or more treatment sessions and only half of all clients referred go on to receive treatment (Richards and Borglin, 2011) with recovery rates of 40 to 46 per cent. Only 8.5 per cent of patients who were unsuccessful in a low intensity intervention then received high intensity CBT. Thus the supervision of a low intensity IAPT worker is likely to have a quite different focus to that of a high intensity worker. A supervisor will need to be able to address major issues: the engagement and retention of clients, making explicit what heuristics are being used for the stepping up of clients for whom a low intensity intervention has been unsuccessful, what type of self-help materials work for which clients under which circumstances. Unfortunately there is very little research that bears on these major issues, and in this uncertainty it is likely that both supervisor and supervisee will themselves use a heuristic such as eminence-based intervention, rather than evidence-based, for example using the self-help materials and computerised packages of the major figures in the field (Lovell and Richards, 2008 and Williams, 2003). The continued use of these products may then be justified using the availability heuristic, e.g. graphically recalling a particular client's very positive response to specific material, then using the representative heuristic to see it as a template for the client's response, preventing experimentation with other materials. This is illustrated in the following exchange:

SUPERVISEE: I found Williams' (2003) five areas approach really useful when I was doing the CBT course and I was pleased when I found it being used in the low intensity IAPT.

SUPERVISOR: It is very useful for teaching students but why would that make it suitable for clients?

SUPERVISEE: I have had good feedback from clients when using it.

SUPERVISOR: So you have got some information that confirms your view of its suitability for clients. What information could you look for that might disconfirm it?

SUPERVISEE: Hmm.

SUPERVISOR: It may be that you are operating with a confirmatory bias (*handing the supervisee Table 2.2*) unwittingly looking for information that confirms your initial supposition but not going on to enquire about information that might disconfirm it.

SUPERVISEE: What might disconfirm it?

SUPERVISOR: Well if you were to ask all clients at the end of treatment, say 'has going through this book helped you deal more effectively with your problems? On a 4-point scale, 4. Yes, it helped a great deal 3. Yes, it helped somewhat 2. No, it really didn't help 1. No, it seemed to make things worse.' This could disconfirm what you initially thought and could open the door to evaluating other self-help materials that are not so much text books for those new to CBT, they may be no better, who knows?

Table 3.1 Motivation/allegiance to CBT ruler

No			Maybe				Yes		
1	2	3	4	5	6	7	8	9	10

The supervisee's work in situations of considerable contextual heterogeneity and supervision has therefore to be appropriately tailored. This therefore requires supervisors to dialogue with would-be supervisees whether they have the skill set and knowledge to conduct their supervision.

Allegiance

Therapists involved in controlled trials of CBT, have been recruited because of an allegiance to CBT. Indeed, as Wampold *et al.* (2010) have pointed out, they would not be regarded as credible CBT trials, without such allegiance. This raises the question of whether, in routine practice, CBT can be delivered without such allegiance. It may be that a would-be supervisee is lukewarm about CBT, but recognises that is where the job opportunities are and so has pursued this avenue. In terms of motivation to practise CBT the supervisee may well be in the action phase as their employer demands, but on the Motivation/Allegiance to CBT Ruler (Table 3.1) they are at say an 8 rather than the 10 the supervisor might assume.

Scores of 1–3 would indicate that a person is pre-contemplative about the practice of CBT, whilst scores of 4–7 would indicate some ambivalence and a perception of advantages and disadvantages, and scores of 8–10 suggest the taking of positive steps to implement CBT. A supervisor with a supervisee that is rated as an 8 has to recognise that the latter could easily slip into the contemplative stage with regard to CBT and may not realise that this has happened. Whilst it is possible to ask supervisees periodically for a recording of a session, the supervisee can choose how to 'perform' for that session, albeit that there are usually some clues in the recording as the following exchange indicates:

SUPERVISOR: Twice in that recording you complimented the client for 'being in touch with his feelings'. What were you trying to convey?

SUPERVISEE: I was just getting him to be sensitive to his gut feeling about his partner's mood when he comes home from work.

SUPERVISOR: Are the gut feelings of an observer a better predictor of someone's mood than the data of behaviours they engage in on a good day, e.g. putting make-up on, washing the breakfast dishes.

SUPERVISEE: Well you have to take account of both.

SUPERVISOR: Which should be given the greater weighting?

SUPERVISEE: Intuition is important.

SUPERVISOR: How does that square with the CBT training?
SUPERVISEE: It is important when dealing with clients with a personality disorder.
SUPERVISOR: Did this client have a personality disorder?
SUPERVISEE: No.

The supervisor has to decide whether and how he/she may work with possible ambivalence.

Chapter 4

Fidelity and flexibility

The goals of CBT supervision include: ensuring translation of the positive results of efficacy trials into routine practice, quality control for the Organisation and facilitating the personal growth and development of the supervisee. But ultimately the economic justification for supervision can only be that it makes a difference to client outcomes. Unfortunately, as indicated in Chapter 1, the case for 'Supervision' per se is, to use the nomenclature of the Scottish Judicial System, 'not proven'. Arguably, making a case for 'Supervision' is akin to attempting to make a case for 'Psychotherapy': the terms cover a multitude of interventions for a wide variety of recipients, so that it is unlikely that the 'Dodo verdict' of 'all are winners and must have prizes' is applicable.

Roth and Fonagy (2005) have argued that with regard to treatment, the important question is 'what treatment works, with which clients, under which circumstances?' For supervision the salient question may be 'which type of supervision works, with which supervisees, under which circumstances? For example supervision may be primarily reflective and developmental or alternatively, psychoeducational and prescribed; supervisees may be experienced or inexperienced, working in high or low intensity IAPT. A fine-grained analysis of the active ingredients in supervision has scarcely begun, but in the meantime given that supervision has been part of the context of the delivery of treatment in controlled trials, it is reasonable that supervision in routine practice should be designed to construct a similar context for the supervisee. This chapter begins with a clarification of the role of the supervisor in randomised controlled trials and the importance attached to ensuring a therapist's faithfulness to manualised procedures. It is argued that such fidelity is also required of a therapist in routine practice, and ways of ensuring this are then discussed. However, the day-to-day context in which some front-line clinicians work is very different to that of the randomised controlled trial, and different ways of monitoring fidelity are elaborated. It is axiomatic that every client is unique and that treatment has therefore to be tailored to the individual, and the next section suggests how this might be achieved without sacrificing fidelity. Because treatment manuals are for the most part diagnosis specific, they necessarily have a limited range of applicability, but in the following section it is argued that with judicious use they are relevant to most clients in routine practice and that without them there are the deleterious consequences of infidelity. In the final section, however, it is recognised that there are areas where evidence based practice is yet to be distilled and the implications for supervision in this context are discussed.

The drama of the Randomised Controlled Trial

Centre stage in an RCT are the therapist and client; practitioners are in the audience and may seek to model their behaviour on that of the therapist. However, the stage production is quite choreographed, the client may or may not approximate to the client seen by the therapist in routine practice. Off stage there is a diagnostician, the script has been written in a manual – albeit like the best actors some ad-libbing (flexibility) is allowed, a supervisor and researchers are ensuring adherence to the protocol (fidelity). The reproduction of the 'on stage' results, in routine practice, may therefore require more than being a 'skilled' practitioner. In transportation from research to practice the role of diagnostician is easily lost and unless the mantle is taken up by the supervisor and supervisee the client may suffer.

If the supervisor Socratically questions the supervisee as to whether their particular client would have been admitted to an RCT for the purported disorder, this can result not only in the redirecting of treatment interventions but also in making the latter aware of heuristics used that lead to inappropriate assessment. The following exchange illustrates the issues that arise:

SUPERVISEE: John has got OCD.
SUPERVISOR: What led you to think that?
SUPERVISEE: Most of the time he goes back and checks that he has locked his car and his front door.
SUPERVISOR: Does he do that to the extent he is late or for a long time?
SUPERVISEE: I don't think so.
SUPERVISOR: What else makes you think he has OCD?
SUPERVISEE: His GP said he has suffered from OCD and depression. At work he has fussed over the type of needle they are using, saying that a needle stick injury is more likely with them; others haven't fussed. I got him to complete this Obsessive Compulsive Inventory and he scored 42, the IAPT cut off is 40.
SUPERVISOR: Could I have a look at the OCI?
SUPERVISEE: Yes (*handing OCI to supervisor*).
SUPERVISOR: I notice his highest scores are for:

I have to review mentally past events, conversations and actions to make sure that I didn't do something wrong
I have saved up so many things that they get in the way
I get upset if objects are not arranged properly
I am excessively concerned about cleanliness

I need things to be arranged in a particular order
I get upset if others change the way I have arranged things

But are there any thoughts or behaviours that are engaged in so much that they interfere with John's functioning?

SUPERVISEE: Well, no, but he is preoccupied about his employer's failure to do anything about the needle.

SUPERVISOR: Has he had a needle stick injury?

SUPERVISEE: Yes, he says they're an occupational hazard as a nurse, but he has now had the all-clear for HIV, Hep B and C. He did see a psychiatrist for OCD years ago and the GP mentioned OCD in the referral.

SUPERVISOR: There is a heuristic called 'Diagnostic Momentum' (Table 2.2) that suggests diagnostic labels once applied get 'stickier' and 'stickier' without critical examination and this may be happening in John's case.

SUPERVISEE: Well what about his score on the OCI?

SUPERVISOR: The 40 cut off suggested by IAPT means that John's score of 42 may suggest OCD but no psychometric test is diagnostic.

SUPERVISEE: Well what is the point of them?

SUPERVISOR: Mainly as a measure of change once you have decided what the person is suffering from.

SUPERVISEE: I was planning that he be stepped up to an OCD programme.

SUPERVISOR: I would hesitate there; perhaps you might use the Health Anxiety Inventory to screen for hypochondriasis and take it from there.

SUPERVISEE: OK.

This exchange illustrates how the supervisor can educate the supervisee on rigorous assessment ensuring that clients are not inappropriately signposted. However, it is not always straightforward as the following dialogue illustrates:

SUPERVISEE: I got John to complete the Health Anxiety Inventory and he scored 18 which is exactly at the cut off IAPT suggest for a diagnosis of hypochondriasis, so where does that leave us?

SUPERVISOR: Could I have a look at his Inventory?

SUPERVISEE: Yes (handing it to therapist)

SUPERVISOR: But 7 of the 18 score are in relation to four items about how he believes he would cope if he did have serious illness; they are not about his functioning now. Does he believe that there is or may well be something seriously wrong with him physically?

SUPERVISEE: No, I don't think so.

SUPERVISOR: I don't think he would be admitted to a trial of CBT for hypochondriasis. Is he depressed?

SUPERVISEE: No, he still goes skiing, plays cards with relatives.

SUPERVISOR: Perhaps consider referring for supportive counselling until he has sorted out the problem with his employer.

This dialogue illustrates that psychometric tests, though useful, can be misleading, resulting in recommendations for unnecessarily intense interventions. An important feature of supervision is to teach supervisees how to benchmark their client against those in controlled trials.

Fidelity

All randomised controlled trials of CBT develop a manual (or in some cases refer to already published sources) that details the treatment intervention. Care is taken that implementation of the CBT manual would be very different to implementation of some comparison condition, e.g. supportive counselling (for which also a treatment manual would be specified). The CBT manuals are disorder/problem specific, i.e. they have different treatment targets and strategies. This manualisation of treatment makes it possible to infer from an RCT which specific CBT protocol is having an effect on which disorder/problem. The manual serves as a reference for therapists, supervisors and researchers involved in the RCT. The CBT pocketbook (Scott, 2011) summarises the treatment targets and strategies for depression and each of the anxiety disorders and is derived from the manuals/publications from the RCTs; it is freely available on http://www. routledgementalhealth.com/simply-effective-group-cognitive-behaviour-therapy-9780415573429, Appendix A. The combination of therapeutic target and treatment strategy is termed by Scott (2009, 2011), a Sat Nav (an aid to treatment direction), for example the Sat Nav for generalised anxiety disorder is shown in Table 4.1.

Thus, in assessing a therapist's adherence to the treatment manual the expectation would be that most of a treatment session would be devoted to most of the targets and strategies in the Sat Nav. Co-morbidity can be addressed by interweaving the Sat Navs for different disorders; examples of this are given in Scott (2009). This can be achieved without any loss of fidelity to individual disorder protocols, just as it is possible to follow a protocol for diabetes and the management of a myocardial infarction in those who have both problems.

In RCTs supervisors check for fidelity by listening to a sample of the supervisee's treatment sessions. Thus in an RCT for generalised anxiety disorder (GAD), if a therapist spent most of a session on, say, activity scheduling or a client's perfectionism, in terms of Table 4.1 a supervisor would question their adherence. The RCTs are not necessarily confined to one principal disorder but are sometimes focussed on a small number of very similar (or comorbid) disorders: for example, the Coping Cat program (Kendall and Hedtke, 2006) is a manual-based CBT for children aged 7 to 13 with generalised anxiety disorder, separation anxiety disorder, and/or social phobia. The treatment is divided into two segments, each of which consists of approximately eight one-hour sessions. The first segment focusses on skills training, whereas the second segment emphasises exposure tasks that place the child in/expose the child to anxiety-provoking situations. To facilitate the learning and recall of several skills, the Coping Cat program presents the

Table 4.1 Generalised anxiety disorder Sat Nav

Therapeutic Targets	Treatment Strategies
1. Beliefs about the uncontrollability of worry	Worry postponement, worry time. Planned ignoring of worries.
2. Beliefs about the danger of worry	
3. Avoidance, reassurance seeking	Openness to all triggers of worry episodes, trusting in own judgement.
4. Thought control strategies	Demonstration of rebound effect of thought suppression.
5. Positive beliefs about worry	Examination of the evidence and counter evidence.
6. Maladaptive metacognitive beliefs about problem solving and intolerance of uncertainty	Problem orientation and effective problem solving.
7. Task interfering cognitions (TIC), Horror video	Switching to task oriented cognitions (TOC) TIC/TOC. Switching to reality video.
8. Perception that demands exceed resources	Working sequentially rather than simultaneously, weaning off excessive responsibility – responsibility pie.
9. Managing mood	Use of MOOD chart.
10. Tension	Applied relaxation.
11. Relapse prevention	Recap of all treatment strategies and distillation of relapse prevention protocol.

steps of anxiety management through the use of an acronym (the FEAR plan). The 'F' step of the FEAR plan, 'Feeling Frightened?' involves identifying bodily reactions that accompany anxiety and gaining an awareness of and control over physiological and muscular anxiety through progressive muscle relaxation. The 'E' step of the FEAR plan, 'Expecting bad things to happen?' involves identifying anxious self-talk and modifying self-talk by considering alternative ways of viewing anxiety-provoking situations. The 'A' step of the FEAR plan, 'Attitudes and Actions that can help,' involves the use of problem-solving to redefine the problem, identify ways to address the problem, and develop a plan to cope with any unwanted distress. Finally, the 'R' step of the FEAR plan, 'Results and Rewards,' involves evaluating and rewarding one's efforts.

Competence is also addressed in RCTs but it is a quite separate matter from adherence. Thus in this example a therapist might skilfully employ Socratic dialogue to challenge a client's perfectionism (a 'competent' performance) but one that is non-adherent. In an RCT it is known by therapists that they would be dropped from the trial for infidelity to the protocol and usually therapists have to demonstrate a certain level of competence to be employed in the trial proper. In routine clinical practice, supervisors rarely check for adherence, but focus instead on assessing competence, i.e. the skill with which a practitioner teaches a skill. However there is no a priori justification for jettisoning a requirement for 'adherence' when transporting the context of an RCT to routine practice.

Fidelity in low intensity interventions

In a review of 13 randomised controlled trial outcome studies of guided self-help (GSH) for depression and the anxiety disorders (Coull and Morriss, 2011), only one study (Lovell *et al.*, 2008) thoroughly addressed the issue of treatment fidelity. Thus there can be no certainty that these treatments were delivered as planned. Furthermore, only six studies provided detail on whether therapists received supervision while guiding the intervention and only five explicitly mentioned that GSH therapists received GSH-specific training prior to applying GSH interventions. Considerable caution is therefore called for in advocating GSH, particularly as Coull and Morriss (2011) found that GSH was of limited effectiveness with clients who were representative of those seen in routine practice. Clients with obsessive compulsive disorder or post-traumatic stress disorder were excluded from the 'anxiety' disorders considered. The Coull and Morriss (2011) study considered a variety of media, including books/manuals/internet.

Treatment fidelity in GSH can be assessed for depression using the freely available self-help manual in Scott (2011) http://www.routledgementalhealth.com/simply-effective-group-cognitive-behaviour-therapy-9780415573429,   by the supervisor completing, Table 4.2 in response to a recording of the session. Table 4.2 is reproduced in Appendix B, together with similar fidelity pro-formas for generalised anxiety disorder, panic disorder and social phobia.

Whilst Table 4.2 does measure adherence in GSH, it also measures the supervisee's skilfulness (competence); as such it is a measure of fidelity rather than adherence alone. Supervisees can also use Table 4.2 as an *aide-memoire* of appropriate foci and as a record of what they did focus on. It is therefore a guide to reflective practice. Clearly discrepancies between the supervisor's view of the degree of fidelity and that of the supervisee can be an important discussion point in the supervision session. Using a similar pro-forma to Table 4.2, Lovell *et al.* (2008) found that whilst therapists generally adhered to the protocol, they often failed to seek feedback on the session. The mean number of sessions was 3.5 and 41 per cent of patients had fewer than 3 sessions, which she and her colleagues regarded as a sub-therapeutic dose of contact.

Table 4.2 Fidelity checklist for depression

Did the therapist focus on this and where applicable its implementation?

Yes (3), Yes, but insufficiently (2), No (1)

1   Assess – using CBT Pocketbook (beginning and end of contact)
2   Psychoeducation – Section 1 How depression develops and keeps going
3   Section 2 No investments, no return
4   Section 3 On second thoughts
5   Section 4 Just make a start
6   Section 5 Expectation versus experience and recalling the positive
7   Section 6 Negative spin or how to make yourself depressed without really trying
8   Section 7 An attitude problem
9   Section 8 My attitude to self, others and the future
10   Section 9 Be critical of your reflex first thoughts not how you feel
11   Section 10 Preventing relapse
12   Collaboratively plan homework
13   Seek feedback on session
14   Clarify if there are further questions
15   Agree next appointment
16   Review homework

The following exchange illustrates the use of Table 4.2 in Supervision:

SUPERVISOR: I listened to your 20-minute tape of your second session. You began reviewing the homework (item 16, Table 4.2), asking whether Jane had gone to bingo and for a swim, which is great, but when she said she didn't, you got hooked into her explanation, 'what will people think about me enjoying myself, they will think I don't care about Alan's death'.

SUPERVISEE: Yes, I think what I was doing was trying to focus on 'Second Thoughts' (item 4, Table 4.2) and get Jane to appreciate that her first thoughts are often overly negative and if she stops and thinks she can come up with better second thoughts.

SUPERVISOR: Yes, I think you did item 4 really well, you used a 'teachable moment' – taking a current concern and using it to illustrate a general principle, this does better ensure that the information is processed and better retained. So for item 4, I rated it a 3 but you didn't use non-completion of homework to illustrate item 3, 'No investment, no return'.

SUPERVISEE: I see what you mean. I missed 'No investment, no return', scored a 1 on this, I think I didn't pursue that direction because she has felt overwhelmed since Alan's death.

SUPERVISOR: If that's the case you could have used item 3, in conjunction with item 5 Just Make A Start. Planning homework would then have involved asking Jane to read Sections 2-4 of the Depression Survival Manual.

SUPERVISEE: Hmm I just asked her to read Section 3 On Second Thoughts.
SUPERVISOR: So for 'Collaboratively Plan Homework', item 12, I rated this a 2.
SUPERVISEE: I do wonder whether Jane should have been referred to GSH.
SUPERVISOR: Was she depressed in terms of the questions in the CBT Pocketbook?
SUPERVISEE: They were not used; the GP completed the PHQ9 and she scored 14 so was put into GSH.
SUPERVISOR: How long is it since her husband died?
SUPERVISEE: 6 months.
SUPERVISOR: She may not actually be depressed and if this is the case a wait and see policy may have been better.

This exchange illustrates some of the dilemmas of low intensity interventions; a desire to increase access by shortening assessments but which can paradoxically increase workloads, leading to a further drive to shorten interventions. Anecdotally, there are problems with staff retention in low intensity interventions with staff wishing to move on to conducting high intensity interventions, often requiring them to seek a post elsewhere. However, there is some evidence that fidelity monitoring can aid staff retention. In a study of evidence-based practice implementation in a children's services system, Aarons *et al.* (2009) found greater staff retention where the evidence-based practice was implemented along with on-going fidelity monitoring presented to staff as supportive consultation. This highlights the need to present fidelity monitoring as a necessary aspect of support rather an imposed organisational demand.

Flexibilty within fidelity

Manualised approaches to treatment are often criticised because they are deemed to take too little account of the individual and their complexities. But if therapists in controlled trials had used the treatment manual as a 'cook book', this would have brought critical comment in Supervision. The expectation is that the treatment interventions flow from the case formulation, which is a specific example of the cognitive model of the disorder. Thus, for example, in an RCT for panic disorder, there would be a focus on catastrophic misinterpretations of bodily sensations with all clients, but for one client the case formulation might involve a belief that in panic they are having a heart attack and always need someone with them for safety whilst for another client the case formulation surrounds their belief of not being able to look after their children or drive safely in the event of a panic attack. The supervisor would expect to learn that the supervisee had tailored the intervention to the specific salient cognitions, i.e. that the therapist had demonstrated what Kendall, Gosch, Furr and Sood (2008) have termed 'flexibility within fidelity'.

There are two poles with regard to treatment: at one extreme is a 'cook book' approach and at the other is a reliance on therapeutic intuition; a manualised approach is located midway between the two extremes. The basis for therapeutic intuition is by definition unclear, but appeal is made to clinical experience and judgement. But clinical prediction has persistently done about 10 per cent less well than mechanical prediction (Grove *et al.*, 2000) and this is particularly the case for clinical judgements based on an interview. Kahneman (2011) gives the example of marital stability being better predicted by a simple formula of frequency of lovemaking minus frequency of quarrels, than by expert judgement. These findings counsel caution if the supervisee is operating near the therapeutic intuition pole, for example when generating formulations, which are known to have low reliability (Kuyken *et al.*, 2005; Kuyken, 2006). A manualised approach imposes checks and balances on clinical judgement without resorting to a 'cook book mentality'.

The following example illustrates that infidelity can involve going outside of a CBT rationale and that there can be instances where adherence should be set aside:

SUPERVISEE: I've been following The Coping Cat programme (Kendall and Hedtke (2006)), with eleven-year-old Joachim, but his behaviour is impossible.

SUPERVISOR: What are his other problems?

SUPERVISEE: He is anxious, worries about everything, he constantly rings his parents when he is out with his friends.

SUPERVISOR: Is he just attention seeking?

SUPERVISEE: That is asking me about his motivation, how can I know that?

SUPERVISOR: Point taken, it is necessarily an arbitrary inference to conclude that someone is attention seeking.

SUPERVISEE: I think seeing Joachim as attention seeking would just put a further barrier between us.

SUPERVISOR: Yes, part of the fidelity to The Coping Cat programme or indeed any CBT programme is staying within the CBT rationale. I was unfaithful in straying into attention seeking.

The above dialogue shows how easy it is for supervisor or supervisee to depart from the CBT rationale described in Chapter One and this is an infidelity that would be unacceptable in an RCT trial of CBT and it is similarly detrimental in routine practice. The supervision session continued:

SUPERVISEE: I had told Joachim he could have a play on my tablet PC at the end of the treatment session. His mother is sitting there with him and he gets up, comes over to me and grabs the input pen out of my hand, mother says in a slightly exasperated tone 'Oh don't be naughty Joachim' and by way of justification then says 'Oh he is like that in school, he's so naughty, the phone goes and I think it will be them again, the school'.

SUPERVISOR: If I was to listen to a CD of your session with Joachim how much of it would be on the content of the Cat Programme and how much on Joachim's misdeeds?

SUPERVISEE: Probably about half.

SUPERVISOR: You might want to consider suspending the Cat Programme and discuss with mum her attending a group parent training programme (see Scott and Stradling, 1987) and then when the behaviour problems become manageable resume the Cat Programme.

This exchange illustrates a flexibility within adherence to programmes, at each stage care is taken that the supervisee is following an empirically supported treatment.

The limitations of treatment manuals

Treatment manuals are not a panacea. For example in the Coping Cat Programme although two out of three youths engaging in the programme significantly reduce their anxiety (Kendall *et al.*, 2012), compared to youth with a principal diagnosis of generalized anxiety disorder (GAD) or separation anxiety disorder (SAD), youth with a principal diagnosis of Social phobia (SP) were more likely to continue to meet criteria for their primary disorder after receiving CBT. This suggests that the Coping Cat Programme had stretched itself too far in trying to cover three disorders and there was a need for a somewhat different intervention for those youth with social phobia. Although a treatment manual based intervention is not invariably effective it is the 'best bet' and should be the treatment of choice.

Despite their evidence base, treatment manuals have not been popular with clinicians in routine practice. Addis and Krasnow (2000) found that 45 per cent of clinicians thought that manuals ignored the unique contributions of therapists and 33 per cent thought that using manuals detracted from the authenticity of the therapeutic interaction. But in fact clients appear happier with manual based intervention (Addis, Wade and Hatgis, 1999). However, it is not known what proportion of practising clinicians have actually tried to use a treatment manual and found them wanting; anecdotally, the author believes that there would be very few.

The disparity between Randomised Controlled Trials and routine practice

It is sometimes contended that research samples are not representative of community samples because the selection criteria of RCTs are not generally inclusive and comorbidity is not highly represented but Stirman, DeRubeis, Crits-Christoph and Rothman (2005) have demonstrated that these differences may be overstated. Stirman *et al.* (2005) mapped charts of individuals seeking treatment under managed care to the criteria of nearly 100 RCTs and identified that 80 per cent of these individuals would be eligible for at least one RCT, and the majority did not have more complex diagnostic profiles than participants included in RCTs. A meta-analysis of 56 effectiveness studies conducted by Stewart and Chambless (2009) gives reasonable confidence that the positive results of randomised controlled trials can be translated to routine practice: large effect sizes were found for panic disorder, post-traumatic stress disorder, generalised anxiety disorder and obsessive compulsive disorder and a medium effect for social anxiety disorder. Overall CBT in routine settings had an improvement of 78 per cent versus 22 per cent for control groups. But although these studies show that efficacious CBT treatments can be translated into routine practice, more recent work suggests that this does not necessarily happen. For example in an effectiveness study of the Coping Cat Programme (Southam-Gerow *et al.*, 2010) using community therapists, the CBT intervention was no better than treatment as usual. Detailed analysis revealed that only 59 per cent of the therapists in the CBT condition reported using exposure tasks. As exposure is the second segment of this programme, this represents not flexibility on the part of therapists but non-adherence to the protocol and arguably inadequate supervision to allow such a state of affairs to develop. In a study of CBT for depression conducted in an outpatient clinic (Gibbons *et al.*, 2010) those with more severe depressive symptoms did less well than in the randomised controlled trials and the authors noted that this may well have been because no fidelity checks were carried out.

The dissemination and implementation (DI) of evidence-based interventions is seen as the major challenge facing the mental health services (see Shafran *et al.*, 2009); in the UK, no more than 10 per cent of people with anxiety or depression receive psychological treatments for their problems and only 5 per cent of the total disorder prevalence had access to an evidence-based psychological treatment (McManus *et al.*, 2009). However, DI should not be seen as a wholly top-down process, supervisors need to be as aware of what 'happens on the ground' in forming judgements about randomised controlled trials. For example Zayfert *et al.* (2005) in a study of the completion of CBT for PTSD in 'real world' clinical practice found that only 28 per cent completed treatment. This echoes the findings of Scott and Stradling (1997) who found that in routine practice only 57 per cent of PTSD clients complied with an audiotape exposure treatment. However, in a community study of refugees using cognitive processing therapy (Schulz, Resick, Huber and Griffin, 2006) the results appeared comparable to those in the PTSD randomised controlled trials but this study involved weekly supervision to ensure reasonable adherence to the CPT protocol. A slight question mark hangs over this study as the authors did not used a 'gold standard' diagnostic assessment, i.e. either the SCID (First *et al.*, 1997) or CAPS (Blake *et al.*, 1990). Tarrier (2001) has observed that the more an RCT trial for PTSD mimics routine practice, the more difficult it is to implement treatment: in the Tarrier *et al.* (1999) study treatment took twice as long as intended because of inconsistent attendance and at follow-up 39 per cent still met criteria for PTSD. Scott (2012) has addressed the difficulties of engaging PTSD clients in routine practice, by describing a non-trauma focussed CBT that has some empirical support and can be used as a stepping stone to trauma focussed CBT and which can also be used as a sole intervention for clients who refuse a trauma focussed intervention. Supervisors have to be cognisant not only of the outcomes of randomised controlled trials but also of what is acceptable in routine practice, i.e. a top-down and bottom-up approach is required.

The consequences of infidelity

In the 56 anxiety disorder effectiveness studies reviewed by Stewart and Chambless (2009), it was found that effect sizes decreased significantly when therapists were not asked to follow a manual and when there was little or no monitoring to make sure the treatment was followed. Stewart and Chambless (2009) assessed the clinical representativeness of the studies they reviewed on a nine-point scale, where points were awarded for clinically representative setting (e.g. outpatient mental health clinic), clinically representative referral (e.g. from GP), clinically representative therapists (e.g. clinicians for whom service is a substantial part of job), clinically representative structure (e.g. treatment with a structure used in clinical practice), clinically representative monitoring (e.g. no formal adherence checks), no pretherapy training (e.g. therapists did not receive special training immediately before study in specific techniques to be used), no randomisation (e.g. clients were not part of a trial), clinically representative patients (e.g. no exclusionary criteria aside from psychosis, suicidality, organic brain disease or substance dependence) and medications allowed. Whilst the study showed that the more representative a study was, the smaller the impact of CBT, the magnitude of the relationship was quite small.

Most of the effectiveness studies considered by Stewart and Chambless (2009) related to individual CBT and though they included group cognitive behaviour therapy (GCBT) effectiveness studies they did not perform a separate analysis for this modality, most probably because there are too few GCBT effectiveness studies at present. In the same year, Oei and Boschen (2009) published a study of the effectiveness of a GCBT programme for clients with a variety of anxiety disorders. Oei and Boschen (2009) concluded that whilst their study demonstrated that treatment was effective in reducing anxiety symptoms to an extent comparable with other effectiveness studies, only 43 per cent of individuals showed reliable change and 17 per cent 'recovered'. Furher Oei and Boschen (2009) claimed that their results were comparable to those found in an effectiveness study of individual CBT conducted by Westbrook and Kirk (2005). The effect sizes in both the Oei and Boschen (2009) and Westbrook and Kirk (2005) studies were less than in efficacy studies conducted in research centres. A UK study of CBT for depression in routine practice (Brown *et al.*, 2011) also showed a sub-optimal outcome, with within subject effect sizes of around 1.0 at post treatment and follow-up both for individual and GCBT. Brown *et al.* (2011) stated 'A standardized treatments manual was not issued, so treatments reflected usual practice in each service'; the absence of a manual makes fidelity to an evidence-based protocol unlikely and the assessment of adherence impossible. Further, the non-use of manuals in 'usual practice' suggests that sub-optimal CBT treatments may be the norm.

In the Oei and Boschen (2009) study it could be that having a variety of anxiety disorder clients in the same group resulted in a less than optimal dose of treatment for each disorder. Whilst the sub-optimal performance in the Oei and Boschen (2009), Westbrook and Kirk (2005) and Brown *et al.* (2011) studies could have arisen because neither used a treatment manual and there was no monitoring to check adherence to a protocol, alternatively the poorer performance could have arisen because of difference between the population/therapists in the research centres and routine practice, the different explanations are not mutually exclusive. Though the precise reason for the lower effect sizes in these studies remains unclear, it seems sensible to use a manualised approach with adherence checks and where possible not to have a mixed group of anxiety disorders.

Fidelity to a manual and adherence checks appear important not only when a particular disorder is the focus but also when a particular difficulty is treated. In a review, anger outcome studies conducted by Di Guiseppe and Tafrate (2003), increased effect sizes were found when manuals and adherence checks were used.

The specific effects of treatment for anxiety and depression in adults have been assessed by Wampold *et al.* (2011), and these authors concluded that though evidence based treatment was superior to a waiting list it was not superior to any active comparison condition. However, in only 8 of the 14 studies analysed were there any adherence checks, and so it cannot be known with any certainty whether an evidence based treatment was in fact delivered.

Evidence-based practice when the evidence base is weak

Although CBT is regarded as the psychological treatment of choice for almost all disorders/difficulties, the supervisor is rather like an engineer and must have an understanding of the limitations of the materials (CBT) he/she is using/ recommending for the contexts in which it is intended to be applied. Whilst the Scientists (CBT Researchers), in some areas, such as depression and the anxiety disorders, have been able to point to a solid evidence base as the foundation for practice, in other areas such as problem gambling (PG) and chronic fatigue syndrome (CFS) the products of their labours are only consensus based recommendations that rely on clinical opinion and expertise. Without an appreciation of the differences in the quality of the evidence base for CBT for different disorders, the supervisor may press for an inappropriate level of adherence to a protocol at the expense of flexibility.

With regard to PG the efficacy studies that have been conducted have involved mainly males; data has only been analysed on those who complete treatment and with short lengths of follow-up. Of the 10 randomised controlled trials seven have been deemed as having a high risk of bias (Bowden-Jones and Smith, 2012). Nevertheless, the guidelines recommend that individual or GCBT, as well as motivational interviewing and motivational enhancement therapy sessions should be delivered in a structured, manualised way by practitioners specifically trained in these forms of treatment (Bowden-Jones and Smith, 2012).

CBT appears somewhat effective for CFS, with 40 per cent of those involved in the randomised controlled trials showing a clinical response to CBT compared to 26 per cent assigned to usual control (Price, Mitchell, Tidy and Hunot, 2008). However, in only 3 of the 15 RCTs reviewed did the researchers report testing treatment fidelity through assessing recording of sessions, thus there could be no certainty that therapists adhered to the CBT model. Further, in only 8 of the 15 studies was a manual or treatment protocol reported to have been used to standardise the CBT intervention.

Thus, where the evidence base for CBT interventions is weak it behoves the supervisor to tread warily and transmit this caution to the supervisee. The following example illustrates some of the difficulties:

SUPERVISEE: I've tried getting Tom to do graded exercise but he just feels worse.

SUPERVISOR: Is that what the CBT protocols are about?

SUPERVISEE: I read them as saying it is about gradually doing more and more, a bit like gradually increasing your fitness to run a half marathon.

SUPERVISOR: I thought it was more about teaching the CFS sufferer to pace themselves working out what they can do day in and day out without an extreme negative reaction where they are out of the game and continuing at that pace independent of your mood.

SUPERVISEE: I must look again at what manuals/protocols I can get hold of.

SUPERVISOR: I would be interested in what you find.

At the next supervision session the dialogue continued:

SUPERVISEE: It's confusing; from what I have read we are both right.

SUPERVISOR: This suggests a lack of clarity with regard to a CBT model of CFS and that up to now it has largely been a matter of let's throw everything at it and hope something sticks.

SUPERVISEE: Where does that leave me?

SUPERVISOR: You are the Engineer, you have found that the material you 'purchased' for Tom does not do the job, and an Engineer would try a different material.

SUPERVISEE: You mean try pacing?

SUPERVISOR: You could do, but there is no guarantee that it will work.

SUPERVISEE: I'll try pacing, but I've also just discovered that because Tom is not getting out and about these days he's into online gambling and this is causing financial and marital problems.

SUPERVISOR: Problem gamblers often have other disorders/difficulties and it is recommended that they be assessed for comorbidity (Bowden-Jones and Smith, 2012).

SUPERVISEE: I don't think he sees the PG as a problem, I don't think he is depressed, it is just the CFS that gets in the way of things.

SUPERVISOR: How could you confirm or deny these speculations?

SUPERVISEE: Maybe I ought to get into some motivational interviewing for the problem gambling?

SUPERVISOR: If you get into treatment before assessment it can be like trying to fix something that is not broken. What proportion of those presenting with problem gambling has it proven possible to engage in CBT?

SUPERVISEE: I don't know.

SUPERVISOR: I'm not sure either, but you should know if perhaps you are tilting at a windmill.

SUPERVISEE: I should look at the problem gambling studies.

SUPERVISOR: That sounds good. I confess, I might have an exaggeratedly negative view of the likelihood of success with clients with an addiction. I just remember vividly some spectacular failures in my own family.

At the next supervision session the exchange continued:

SUPERVISEE: I couldn't find any clear data on the levels of engagement of problem gamblers in CBT.

SUPERVISOR: Researchers should present an intention to treat analyses but don't and it can give a mistaken idea about the acceptability of an intervention.

In the above dialogues the supervisor has been intent on making the supervisee hyper-vigilant when operating in areas where the CBT evidence base is weak. But the supervisor has also been alert that his/her own CDRs (the availability heuristic Table 2.2) could more easily colour his/her suggestions in such an area of uncertainty.

Chapter 5

The supervisory context

Supervision in randomised controlled trials is a carefully controlled process, in which the supervisor performs a quality control process ensuring fidelity to a treatment manual for the particular disorder/difficulty under investigation. With such monitoring it is unsurprising, that usually, no therapist effects on treatment outcome are found (e.g. Cella *et al.*, 2011). Further, the investigators (the Organisation) in RCTs are wholly committed to the full implementation of the different arms of the study, e.g. CBT vs. treatment as usual. Evidence-based treatments (EBTs) can, however, become very diluted by the time they reach routine practice. This chapter begins with a discussion of the determinants of evidence-based practise (EBP) and then suggests that training can be insufficient to ensure that EBTs are not attenuated. EBTs can be likened to a signal of a certain strength and in the following section the supervisor's role is to maintain signal strength as an advocate of EBTs. Continuing the technical metaphor in the following section the supervisee's role is conceptualised as an 'engineer' – learning how to perform particular tasks, learning how to solve particular problems, learning about new approaches relevant to their particular tasks and acquiring and expanding background knowledge helpful to the performance of their tasks. This contrasts with the role of 'scientists' who are mandated to obtain specific answers to their own research and writing. The final section of this chapter is devoted to organisational mandates operating on front-line clinicians.

Factors in the delivery of services at the coalface

The set-up in RCTs represents a particular synergy of client, therapist/supervisee, supervisor and Organisation, and the more general interactions of these factors are shown in Figure 5.1.

Figure 5.1 shows that a therapist/supervisee is likely to be highly (thickest arrows) influenced by their training, by the Organisation in which they are working and by their supervision. To usually a very limited degree (single arrows), the therapist can influence their Organisation and perhaps also their training. The therapist/supervisee is likely to have a somewhat greater influence (the double-headed arrows) on their supervisor. There may also be reciprocal interactions

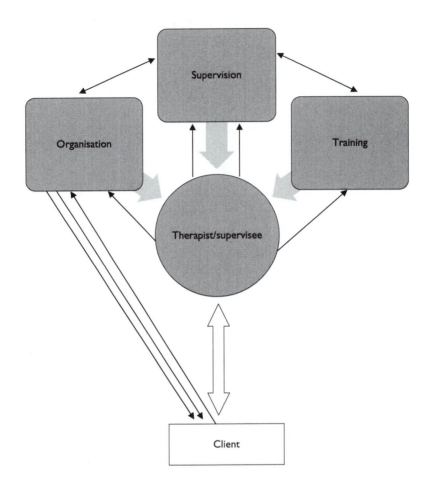

Figure 5.1 Determinants of evidence-based practice.

(single double-headed arrows) between the Organisation, supervisor and Training. The client may influence (single arrow) the Organisation by providing feedback on satisfaction with therapy but the Organisation is likely to exert a more powerful influence (double-headed arrows) on the client, specifying the number of treatment sessions available and their format, e.g. individual or group. Organisations may have varying degrees of commitment to EBT or differing definitions as to what constitutes EBT. The client can exert a major influence on the therapist, for example if they are suffering from a disorder outside the range of expertise of the therapist or from a disorder for which EST is weak, e.g. chronic fatigue syndrome. Similarly if the therapist is adhering to an appropriate EBT there will be a major influence on the client.

Given the more general model of the interactions of client, therapist/supervisee and Organisation shown in Figure 5.1, it should come as no surprise that outcomes in routine practice can differ markedly from those in the RCTs. For example, Wiborg *et al.* (2012) explored the role of the context on treatment outcome in manualised CBT for chronic fatigue syndrome outside specialised treatment settings. They found that equally well trained therapists produce different outcomes. The effect of the therapist accounted for 21 per cent of the total variance in post-treatment fatigue. Wiborg *et al.* (2012) also found that a stronger belief that treatment manuals threaten the freedom and flexibility of therapists seemed to be related to less effective treatments.

A supervisor's advocacy of fidelity and flexibility can be facilitated or impeded by the training of the supervisee and the expectations of the employing Organisation. Without an appreciation of the possible operation of countervailing forces the supervisor may overestimate the likely impact of his/her central messages, as the following dialogue illustrates:

SUPERVISOR: What resources have you drawn upon to guide your helping Tina?
SUPERVISEE: Well she has an eating disorder and my formulation is that she equates her worth with her appearance and so we are doing cognitive restructuring.
SUPERVISOR: Which eating disorder is it, anorexia, bulimia?
SUPERVISEE: I don't think it is bulimia, but I am taking a transdiagnostic approach.
SUPERVISOR: Based on what?
SUPERVISEE: On my formulation.
SUPERVISOR: Why?
SUPERVISEE: Formulation is critical, it is what we were taught on the course, Padesky (1996) and all that.
SUPERVISOR: Do you get Tina to keep a diary of what she eats and any compensatory behaviour such as excessive exercise or vomiting?
SUPERVISEE: Not exactly but I've a good idea of what she does.
SUPERVISOR: Do you get her to complete a Thought Record?
SUPERVISEE: No, we talk around key cognitions.
SUPERVISOR: How do you know which ones are key?
SUPERVISEE: It's back to my formulation.

In this exchange it has become apparent that the supervisee's training has given a pre-eminence to the idea of formulation and that following a protocol is inappropriate. The above dialogue reflects the findings of Waller *et al.* (2012) who in a study of 80 qualified clinicians who offered what they described as CBT for adults with eating disorders found that the implementation of specific CBT techniques was far lower than protocols would suggest. However, the use of treatment manuals was associated with greater use of recommended CBT techniques. Waller *et al.* (2012) concluded that stronger training and closer supervision of clinicians was necessary to give clients the best chance of recovery. Interestingly, implementation of specific CBT techniques was far lower than protocols would suggest for those *more* experienced in working with the eating disorders, anxious and older clinicians. They added that clinicians' use of the label CBT is not a reliable indicator of the therapy that is being offered.

At the next supervision session, the dialogue with the supervisee continued:

SUPERVISOR: I was curious about your reference to Padesky (1996) at the last session and so I went back and looked at her writings. In her chapter in *The Frontiers of Cognitive Therapy* (1996) she wrote (*handing a copy to the supervisee*):

> two possible criteria for therapist competency are knowledge of and adherence to treatment protocols . . . the development of specific cognitive therapy protocols for specific disorders assumes that protocol adherence is linked to therapy outcome . . . Guided discovery is the engine that drives client learning in cognitive therapy. Treatment protocols are followed as closely as ideal for a particular client's treatment . . . Another cornerstone of cognitive therapy instruction is teaching therapists to formulate a useful conceptualization. . . . Much of the time, however, clients present with more than one difficulty requiring the therapist to combine or choose among generic conceptual models . . . Students are encouraged to experiment with diagnostically based conceptualizations, written case conceptualization forms . . . and diagrams of client patterns to discover which approaches are most helpful.

What do you make of that?

SUPERVISEE: It's not quite what I remember of her work on the CBT course, I need to mull it over at home and come back to you on this.

It is unclear from the above exchange whether the supervisee's initial take on Padesky's work reflects how it was presented on his/her training course or whether it represents the supervisee's idiosyncratic take of the course. Nevertheless the supervisor is concerned to understand the rationales that govern the supervisee's work and to enable her/him to critically examine them.

Training can be insufficient to translate EBTs into routine practice

In a review of the role of therapist training in the implementation of psychosocial treatments Herschell *et al.* (2010) found that neither reading a manual, self-directed training or workshops routinely produce positive outcomes, albeit that workshop follow-ups help to sustain outcomes. Even when there is specific evidence-based training of therapists the results may not translate into routine practice. For example, Feigenbaum *et al.* (2012) in a study of 'Dialectical Behaviour Therapy for Cluster B Personality Disorders' in routine practice, provided extensive DBT training for the therapists. The therapists recruited for the study were three clinical psychologists and two senior community psychiatric nurses. The therapists were asked to read and discuss a treatment manual and then had two days' training in the UK from a DBT trainer. This was followed by two five-day intensive training courses six months apart in the USA. In addition there was a day a year of expert consultation. All therapists attended weekly DBT consultation and skills development meetings (2.5 hours) and received individual peer supervision. However, there was no formal assessment in supervision of whether the protocol was actually being implemented. But adherence to the model was monitored by the team through weekly case discussion, verbal reporting of session content and listening to each other's audio tapes. Both the DBT and Treatment As Usual groups improved on a range of measures; however, the TAU group showed comparable reductions in all measures and a larger decrease in para-suicidal behaviours and risk. The authors commenting on the study reflected that no member of the team received supervision from an adherent DBT therapist. They justified this by stating that in routine practice adherence is not routinely monitored, but arguably it ought to be. But problems with adherence may be only one of a number of reasons for the disappointing results in this study; other reasons include that the study was not restricted to females or clients with a borderline personality disorder, BPD (28 per cent of the clients had an anti-social personality disorder).

More generally the training of supervisees may have been insufficient to make them informed consumers of evidence. Whilst it would not be the intent of most CBT courses to make the students researchers, as 'engineers' rather than 'scientists' they should be able to distinguish the best from the worst evidence. Thus there should be a basic familiarity with statistical and methodological concepts, not the capacity to apply them to research design. The supervisee should be able to, or be helped to, operate with a clear distinction between efficacious and possibly efficacious treatments (see Appendix C Chambless and Hollon, 1998). The goal of teaching evidence-based practice is to install a 'crap detector' (Bilsker and Goldner, 1999) and part of the installation is creating an awareness of the quality of the comparison conditions (if any) when any intervention has been evaluated. The zeitgeist on some courses is that an emphasis on evidence may be too narrow and unfeeling, overly focussed on quantitative data, ignoring the human context of mental health problems. This can generate amongst students a wariness of being drawn into a detached number crunching, dehumanising style of practice. One way of circumventing this is for the supervisor to ask the supervisee to identify a client with a particular problem and ask them to undertake a search of the literature and decide on a course of action integrating research and clinical information. The use of such problem-based learning roots the evidence-based literature in a real-life clinical context and best illustrates its compassionate use. Material on evidence-supported treatments is more likely to be processed and retained by the supervisee when it addresses a current problem.

The supervisor as advocate of EBTs

In order for EBTs to be translated into routine practice, the supervisor has to facilitate the supervisee's passage through five main steps, shown in Figure 5.2: knowledge, persuasion, decision, implementation and confirmation (the innovation–decision process described by Rogers (2003)); in practice the steps somewhat overlap.

Supervisees are likely to vary enormously in their openness to travelling along the pathways shown in Figure 5.2, and may become stuck at any point in the process. Gallo and Barlow (2012) have pointed out that this openness is not likely to be an all or nothing phenomenon but that there may be some EBT interventions that a therapist is more open to than others. Ultimately it is the supervisee who chooses to implement and stay with an EBT but the supervisor is a catalyst in the process.

Figure 5.2 requires that both supervisor and supervisee endeavour to keep abreast of the research literature; it is likely to be too onerous a task for either alone. But this endeavour can be sabotaged if either believes the literature is of little or no relevance. In principle, workshops and conferences provide a means of keeping up to date with developments, but can often consist of luminaries marketing their wares, with no indication of the evidence for the added value of the intervention over existing methods. Without an empirical stance supervisees in particular can fall prey to novelty in the guise of professional development.

Whilst a supervisor is a collaborator with the supervisee, he/she is also in the role of persuader (see Figure 5.2) with regards to EBTs. In this connection supervisors may find it useful to draw upon the Elaboration Likelihood Model of Persuasion, which makes a distinction between central processing in which the details of the argument are effortfully processed and peripheral processing in which a rule of thumb is used by-passing central processing: for example a supervisee doing what a

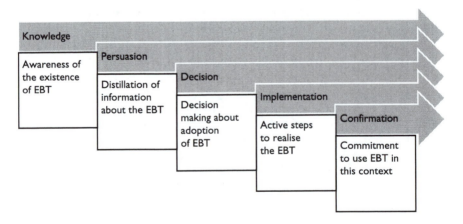

Figure 5.2 From outcome study to routine practice utilising the innovation–decision process.

supervisor says because of their authority rather than being convinced of the evidence evinced. The ELM model (Petty and Cacioppo, 1986) suggests that lasting change only occurs when information is centrally processed. Thus in terms of Figure 5.2, though a supervisee might decide on a particular intervention and the steps necessary to implement it there may not be 'confirmation' in using this approach in this context and the supervisee may be prone to therapeutic drift. The following exchange highlights the difficulties in moving through Figure 5.2:

SUPERVISOR: I was thinking about your client with an eating disorder. There's the *Cognitive Therapy for Eating Disorders* book by Glenn Waller and colleagues (2007).
SUPERVISEE: You mean Tina. I'm not sure whether her low self-esteem came before or after her eating disorder, so I don't know whether the eating disorder should be the target.
SUPERVISOR: But the CBT eating disorder treatment models target low self-esteem whether this occurred pre or post eating disorder.
SUPERVISEE: I was thinking of the Melanie Fennell (1999) workshop on low self-esteem and just following this.
SUPERVISOR: But there is no evidence that it is a stand-alone treatment for eating disorder?
SUPERVISEE: Well maybe not yet!

In this dialogue the supervisor's message about using an EBT for eating disorders is not being centrally processed by the supervisee, rather the latter has used an idiosyncratic formulation that asserts focus on low self-esteem if this predates the eating disorder. The exchange continued:

SUPERVISOR: Looking back at the Summary of Padesky's work I gave you last session, how does your approach to Tina fit into this?
SUPERVISEE: Well I can see where you are coming from in suggesting a manualised treatment from the first part of what Padesky (1996) said, but the last part of what she said

Much of the time, however, clients present with more than one difficulty requiring the therapist to combine or choose among generic conceptual models . . . Students are encouraged to experiment with diagnostically based conceptualizations, written case conceptualization forms . . . and diagrams of client patterns to discover which approaches are most helpful

justifies my approach.
SUPERVISOR: What is the evidence base for the second half of Padesky's statement, that there should be reliance on generic conceptual models?
SUPERVISEE: Well she said it!
SUPERVISOR: Does that make it true?

SUPERVISEE: Well, no.

SUPERVISOR: What is the evidence that if a client has more than one difficulty a generic approach is required?

SUPERVISEE: I don't know of any.

SUPERVISOR: What is the evidence that generic CBT works?

SUPERVISEE: None that I know of.

SUPERVISOR: Perhaps the nearest tests of a generic CBT are the trials of Brown *et al.* (2011) and Westbrook and Kirk (2005), as they did not use manuals and there was no diagnostic assessment based on a structured interview. The results were significantly less impressive than in comparable efficacy studies. Have you tried Waller's manual (2007) for eating disorders?

SUPERVISEE: No.

SUPERVISOR: How can you know whether manuals restrict your freedom without experimenting with them?

SUPERVISEE: I just find it easier to use formulations.

SUPERVISOR: If I told you that the protocol for resuscitation for the general public is make sure you are safe, get someone to ring an ambulance, take the person by the shoulders, if they are unresponsive to what you are saying put your head close to their mouth and if you can't feel their breath or see their chest rising and falling begin compressions at 100 a minute, and somebody decided to do their own thing, e.g. throwing cold water over them, giving them a hug, what would you think?

SUPERVISEE: I don't like to medicalise clients, it's different if it is something like resuscitation.

SUPERVISION: In terms of accountability is it acceptable to do anything other than an evidence-based intervention?

The above dialogue illustrates how discussion of evidence-based protocols can be short circuited by an appeal to clinical freedom. Mercier and Sperber (2011) have hypothesised that the function of reason is not to establish objective truth but to find easily justified reasons for current behaviour that might persuade others, and the appeal to clinical freedom may be such an example. Alternatively the initial jettisoning of treatment manuals by the supervisee in the above example may be an example of the loss aversion bias operating, in that the supervisee is averse to the loss of freedom. If it is the case that a loss aversion bias operates with regard to clinical freedom then there may be a need to stress the positive benefits of using a manual, e.g. 'using a CBT manual for PTSD can ensure at least 50 per cent recovering, without it there are no guarantees at all'.

The supervisee as an engineer

The processes involved in Figure 5.2 parallel those of a supervisee, conceptualised as an engineer, guided by the steps in Figure 5.3 – the '5As' from Spring and Neville (2011).

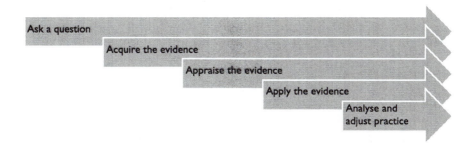

Figure 5.3 The supervisee as an engineer.

The following example illustrates the usage of Figure 5.3.

SUPERVISEE: After our last session I looked at Padesky's (1996) statement that 'Guided discovery is the engine that drives client learning in cognitive therapy' but where is the evidence on this?

SUPERVISOR: I suppose there must be evidence but I can't think what! Perhaps we should acquire (see Figure 5.3) the evidence for next time and then look at how it stacks up?

SUPERVISEE: OK.

At the next supervision session the dialogue continued:

SUPERVISOR: I was surprised not to come up with anything, other than some general stuff that cognitive change seems to precede changes in emotion, but that does not really address how cognitive change comes about.

SUPERVISEE: I found this in Scott (2009):

Whilst therapist competence (as measured by the Cognitive Therapy Rating Scale) has been found to relate to outcome in cognitive therapy for depression (Shaw *et al.*, 1999), the effect is modest, accounting for just 19 per cent of the variance in outcome on a clinician administered measure and with no relation with self-report outcome measures. Further the aspect of competence that was most associated with outcome was structure (this referred to setting an agenda, assigning relevant homework and pacing the session appropriately) by contrast general therapeutic skills or specific CBT skills did not predict outcome. It is not clear whether there would be similar findings for other disorders. Further it could be that the Cognitive Therapy Rating Scale is a poor measure of competence, nevertheless the CTRS in its original or updated form tends to be the 'gold standard' for assessing CBT students and practitioners across the range of common mental health disorders. The Shaw *et al.* (1999) study should at least caution against an overemphasis on skill at the expense of structure – setting a homework at the end of sessions (including the first) would seem of key importance

so there does not look like there is evidence that Guided Discovery is key.

SUPERVISOR: It certainly looks like a stronger case can be made for agenda and homework.

SUPERVISEE: I can't remember much being said about homework on my training course, it's the Socratic dialogue that sticks out.

SUPERVISOR: Was it suggested that you write down the homework in a way that summarises the session?

SUPERVISEE: No.

SUPERVISOR: Given that patients generally have poor recall of what their Doctor has said, because of anxiety, how likely is it that clients will faithfully recall what is said in a therapy session, much less act on it between sessions?

In the above exchange the supervisor and supervisee have collaboratively appraised the evidence, Figure 5.3 and the next steps are to apply it and adjust practice in the light of experience. At the next Supervision session the dialogue continued:

SUPERVISOR: How did you get on writing the client's homework down?

SUPERVISEE: I just jotted down some reminders of the session for them.

SUPERVISOR: So it wasn't like the equivalent of a 'prescription' for them, do 'x' and 'y' and we can review how it works out?

SUPERVISEE: No.

SUPERVISOR: When you saw the client next time was there a focus on these 'reminders'?

SUPERVISEE: No, I didn't have a copy of what I had written down for them.

SUPERVISOR: So you had no written reference session to session to ensure continuity between sessions.

SUPERVISEE: No.

SUPERVISOR: So you haven't actually addressed homework?

SUPERVISEE: No, but I have possibly taken a first step.

SUPERVISOR: I remembered to ask you about the 'homework' because I have written down that it was a focus at our last session. There doesn't appear to be anything in your record keeping that ensures continuity, follow through.

SUPERVISEE: Well, I write down whether the client is making use of the sessions, whether they are feeling better, what has happened since the last session.

SUPERVISOR: But what is there in the records in terms of accountability, that would enable the Organisation to say that in this session there is evidence that an evidence-based skill was taught and procedures were put in place to review and refine acquisition of that skill?

SUPERVISEE: I hadn't thought of the records in terms of accountability.

SUPERVISOR: I think with GP commissioning, questions are going to be asked by GPs about 'what am I paying for?' Unless an Organisation can meaningfully answer this they will likely be dropped as a provider.

In this dialogue the supervisor and supervisee have refined the final stage in Figure 5.3, adjustment to practice, but in so doing account has also been taken of the wider organisational context of supervision, Figure 5.1. Throughout the supervision sessions the supervisor has also been mindful of the training influences operating on the supervisee. Both organisational and training aspects can facilitate or inhibit EST; however, if the supervisee is mindful of the 5 As they are better able to distill the best and worst of both and adjust practice accordingly, as a good 'engineer' would.

Organisational mandates

Organisations may be commissioned to provide a particular service, for example guided self-help (GSH), a Pain Management Programme or an Eating Disorder Intervention. A supervisor working in such contexts is then under pressure to see that the 'product' of the Organisation is delivered, i.e. that there is adherence to the prescribed protocols. But clients may have or develop co-morbid disorders that are not catered for by the protocols and the client's attendance at the service may be threatened or curtailed, despite a comprehensive service being unavailable elsewhere. The supervisor can play a role in helping to ensure that a supervisee develops sufficient breadth of skills to address all the problems that the client is complaining of. Zimmerman and Mattia (2000) have established that clients want treatment for all their difficulties.

In these circumstances the supervisor and supervisee must retain the critical stance embodied in Figure 5.3, asking questions for example about whether the apparently cheaper GSH can deliver in practice and whether a narrow focus on, say, Pain Management will be applicable to clients with, say, co-existing PTSD. This awareness of the said limitations of the intervention can put the supervisor (and indeed the supervisee) at loggerheads with Management who may or may not be clinicians.

In this section the role of the supervisor in helping the supervisee manage organisational mandates in three contexts (i) low intensity CBT (ii) Pain Management and (iii) an Eating Disorder Unit is considered.

(i) Low intensity CBT

The organisational difficulties of supervising in a low intensity CBT context are highlighted in the following exchange:

SUPERVISEE: The Charity I work for has just got the IAPT low intensity contract, but I'm not sure how many of the people we see are really suitable for low intensity work.

SUPERVISOR: How do you assess suitability?

SUPERVISEE: Well it is for mild to moderate anxiety and depression.

SUPERVISOR: How do you establish whether a client falls into these categories?

SUPERVISEE: Well if they have a PHQ9 score of 10 or over that is depression and according to IAPT, 10–14 is moderate and 15–19 is moderately severe, so it should exclude those with 20 and above. A GAD7 score of 8 or over is anxiety and 15 or over is severe anxiety. But most of our clients are in the severe range on these measures.

SUPERVISOR: It does seem a bit of an arbitrary way of selecting people.

SUPERVISEE: Well you do ask as well 'are they depressed and down most of the day most days?' to signpost depression and 'do you worry uncontrollably?' to signpost anxiety. But still there are not many for whom the low intensity is appropriate.

SUPERVISOR: Perhaps the low intensity is really intended for all comers and they are then stepped up to high intensity if unsuccessful?

SUPERVISEE: But we don't have a contract to provide high intensity work, they would have to be referred on again to the team at the local Hospital.

SUPERVISOR: What is wrong with that?

SUPERVISEE: I think that many might not bother, but I think it is a numbers game from our Management.

SUPERVISOR: Maybe we need to look at the good you can do where you are.

SUPERVISEE: I can certainly think of a few people who have responded very positively to GSH.

SUPERVISOR: Maybe you will need to keep them in mind to motivate yourself, I must have a look at the evidence base on GSH.

This dialogue illustrates how a supervisee can feel powerless in the face of organisational demands and the supervisor can catch much of the same sense of powerlessness. But by asking a question, the first step of Figure 5.3, about the effectiveness of GSH, a way forward may be indicated. The exchange continued at the next session:

SUPERVISOR: I looked up a paper by Coull and Morriss (2011) on the clinical effectiveness of CBT-based guided self-help and their conclusion was that although there is support for the effectiveness of CBT-based GSH among media-recruited individuals they found that the reviewed randomised controlled trials had limited effectiveness within routine clinical practice and there is a paucity of evidence on longer-term outcomes.

SUPERVISEE: What type of clients were they?

SUPERVISOR: These were clients with mild to moderate anxiety and depression and Coull and Morriss (2011) found 13 studies on which to base their conclusions.

SUPERVISEE: So the CBT-based GSH is actually a 'definite maybe'.

SUPERVISOR: You could put it like that.

SUPERVISEE: At least I won't have unrealistic expectations of what I'm doing.

SUPERVISOR: It could stop you automatically personalising it if a client is unresponsive and stop you getting demoralised.

SUPERVISEE: That's good.

In this exchange the supervisee has picked up the baton from the supervisor's initial question and exposition of the evidence to complete the final three stages of Figure 5.3. The supervisee has thus been taught to better manage the organisational stresses, by an appreciation of the possible limits of the intervention used. However, this is not to say that adherence to a protocol is not also required in low intensity interventions (see Chapter 4).

(ii) Pain Management

Pain Management Programmes are usually run in specialised centres but supervisees working in more general settings often encounter clients with pain in addition to some other difficulty such as post-traumatic stress disorder, both conditions arising from a trauma. This can present organisational problems as the following dialogue illustrates:

SUPERVISEE: Alan is reminded of the explosion at work by the pain he is in. He fell as he ran out of the factory injuring his right knee. My Manager thinks I should refer him to the Pain Management Centre and the Orthopaedic Surgeon has also recommended this, so reluctantly Alan went along for an assessment and he wasn't impressed when he learnt treatment would involve attendance at a group four days a week for three weeks.

SUPERVISOR: Why is that a problem?

SUPERVISEE: Part of his PTSD is that he cuts himself off from others and is very irritable, I can't see them handling him or him them.

SUPERVISOR: I'm not familiar with Pain Management Programmes. Why not do a literature search on it, Google CBT Pain Management and see whether Alan is an appropriate candidate or whether something else might be appropriate?

SUPERVISEE: OK.

In this exchange the supervisor has acknowledged his/her gaps in his/her knowledge base thereby encouraging the supervisee that there can also be gaps in the latter's knowledge. But that it is possible to plug these gaps by making an evidence-based enquiry and relating the findings to the needs of a particular client. Because the enquiry is germane to the supervisee's current concern, learning is likely to be maximised and retained. At the next supervision session the following dialogue took place:

SUPERVISEE: I came across a review of CBT for pain by Morley, Eccleston and Williams (2000): they considered biofeedback/relaxation, behaviour therapy and CBT and found that CBT was best. But the studies were predominantly focussed on chronic low back pain and arthritis so I'm not sure that a Pain Management Programme based on such studies is going to be relevant to Alan.

SUPERVISOR: I can see your point.

SUPERVISEE: It also said that 76 per cent of CBT treatment studies for pain have been group based, so you don't know how much group processes have contributed to the results, as opposed to the specific CBT strategies employed.

SUPERVISOR: Can I have a look at the paper? I see they summarised the results of 25 studies (*as in Table 5.1*).

An effect size is a measure of the difference between the effects of a treatment and a comparison condition (it is calculated by subtracting the end of treatment mean (e.g. for CBT) from the mean at the end of the comparison condition (which could for example be a waiting list control condition) and dividing by the standard deviation (a measure of the spread of scores)). Effect sizes of 0.2 are regarded as small, 0.5 medium and 0.8 is large. Thus in Table 5.1 for the different aspects of pain, the effect sizes are averaging around 0.5 (middle column) when CBT and a waiting list are compared, i.e. there is a medium effect. However, when CBT is compared to some active condition (a mix of symptom monitoring, bibliotherapy and physiotherapy), in only three of the eight dimensions of pain considered are there statistically significant differences and even then for two of the three the effect size is small.

Table 5.1 Psychological treatment v Waiting List Control (WLC) and Active Treatment Control (ATC)

	Treatment v WLC	Treatment v ATC
Domain	Mean effect size	Mean effect size
Pain experience	0.40 (0.22 to 0.58)	0.29 (0.11 to 0.46)
Mood or affect (depression)	0.36 (0.13 to 0.59)	−0.14 (−0.32 to 0.04)*
Mood or affect (other)	0.52 (0.19 to 0.84)	0.05 (−0.27 to 0.37)*
Cognitive coping and appraisal (negative)	0.50 (0.27 to 0.73)	0.17 (−0.08 to 0.42)*
Cognitive coping and appraisal (positive)	0.53 (0.28 to 0.78)	0.40 (0.21 to 0.62)
Behavioural expression of pain	0.50 (0.22 to 0.78)	0.27 (0.08 to 0.47)
Increased behaviour activity	0.46 (0.25 to 0.72)	—
Social role functioning	0.60 (0.44 to 0.76)	0.17 (−0.08 to 0.34)*

Source: Morley, Eccleston and Williams (2000)

* Not significant.

SUPERVISEE: It doesn't seem to make a case for interrupting Alan's PTSD treatment and sending him off to Pain Management.

SUPERVISOR: No, I will have a look at the literature myself and come back to you on this.

In this dialogue both supervisor and supervisee are collaborating to answer the question 'is traditional CBT Pain Management appropriate for a PTSD client?', and are moving through the 5As of Figure 5.3. At the next supervision session the supervisor adds further evidence:

SUPERVISOR: I came across a follow-up paper, Eccleston, Williams and Morley (2009) to the one you brought in, and the number of studies considered this time had gone up to 40, but none of the studies are specifically of clients suffering pain from extreme trauma. The authors concluded 'CBT may have a weak effect in improving pain, mood and disability in adults with chronic pain'.

SUPERVISEE: From what I can gather the Pain Management Programmes seem to be a generic CBT and the only unique emphasis is teaching clients to pace themselves and not to catastrophise; these strategies are explained in the Self-help book *Moving On After Trauma*, Scott (2009).

SUPERVISOR: Yes. I can see no reason why you should not integrate these strategies into your PTSD treatment of Alan.

SUPERVISEE: But my Line Manager may well say that the Orthopaedic Surgeon has recommended the Pain Management Programme and the Organisation will want to go with that.

SUPERVISOR: Hmm, eminence based rather than evidence based. Perhaps you might try out these strategies whilst Alan is on the waiting list for the Pain Management Programme and get him to read about them, then he can decide.

SUPERVISEE: OK.

The above dialogue illustrates that the supervisee is not a free agent in the delivery of CBT and that there can be significant organisational constraints (Figure 5.1), but in collaboration with the supervisor these are not necessarily insuperable. Further, by championing ESTs the supervisee gains an increased freedom.

(iii) Eating Disorder Unit

Contracts between Commissioning bodies and Providers sometimes specify a particular client population, for example clients with eating disorders, but this can be problematic as clients may present with multiple disorders and wish for treatment for all their disorders (Zimmerman and Mattia, 2000). Further, difficulties may arise during the course of treatment that may raise questions, particularly from line managers, about whether the Specialised Unit is the appropriate treatment setting. Therapists/supervisees may act as a conduit for the organisational concerns, presenting them in Supervision, as the following example illustrates:

SUPERVISEE: I'm fed up. I didn't attend a staff meeting, because I wanted to squeeze in an appointment with Maxine: she's got anorexia and Borderline Personality Disorder, but has recently been diagnosed with breast cancer. My line manager asked me why I missed the meeting and I told her, she just said we need to talk about time management sometime. I was furious, the staff meetings just go on and on, with people who like the sound of their own voices.
SUPERVISOR: Did you tell your manager this?
SUPERVISEE: No, I just fumed; talking to her is just like talking to the wall!

This exchange illustrates how a therapist's difficulties would be magnified if a line manager was also a supervisor. A supervisor provides an opportunity for the supervisee to express distressing emotion generated by organisational factors. The dialogue continues:

SUPERVISEE: My line manager thinks Maxine should be discharged from our Service to attend some Breast Cancer Support Group and be re-referred back to us if necessary, but we were just beginning to get somewhere. She was eating more. I'm not saying it was all down to me. Since having the baby she is more motivated.
SUPERVISOR: Would it be a bad idea for her to attend a Support Group?
SUPERVISEE: She's frightened, feels she makes a mess of relationships, gets close and then does a runner.
SUPERVISOR: Classic borderline personality disorder.
SUPERVISEE: So I wouldn't want to push her; if she wants to give it a go fine, but she does need a safe place from which to operate.
SUPERVISOR: And you have become the 'Safe Place'?
SUPERVISEE: I guess.
SUPERVISOR: But the trouble seems to be the Organisation sees itself as treating eating disorders, not as a sanctuary.
SUPERVISEE: We have got to do both, it can't be so narrow. If Maxine is discharged she will see it as abandonment and the anorexia will worsen.
SUPERVISOR: My guess is that the breast cancer is going to heighten anorexic issues and there is even more reason for her staying within the Service. Speaking from my own experience of breast cancer I still feel the terror of recurrence. A woman's identity is bound up with her breasts, people treat you differently before you have breasts to afterwards and I confess I feel ashamed about feeling ashamed of my breast reconstruction.
SUPERVISEE: Oh thanks for that, it is what I surmised somehow.
SUPERVISOR: I think that though we do have to keep to ESTs for eating disorders it doesn't mean we don't also pay attention to our gut reactions and experiences.

SUPERVISEE: I guess it is a matter of balancing the two. But how do I retain Maxine in the Service?

SUPERVISOR: You could suggest to your line manager that she could discharge Maxine but that Maxine will be asking for immediate re-referral by her GP.

SUPERVISEE: She might report me to her manager.

SUPERVISOR: At that point I would write a letter to the manager detailing our discussion in supervision.

This dialogue illustrates that on occasion the supervisor may have to influence the Organisation (see Figure 5.1) in order to assist the supervisee. Further, the supervisor is not seated as the fount of all wisdom simply espousing evidence-based interventions but is also calling on and using her own personal experience to work collaboratively with the supervisee towards ensuring a better outcome for the client.

Fidelity and flexibility in training

CBT training courses in the UK emphasise the acquisition of competence in order to achieve client outcomes. Much emphasis is placed on the videoing of treatment sessions and the rating of competence displayed using the Cognitive Therapy Rating Scale and the importance of a formulation of the client's difficulties. The emphasis is usually heavily loaded to the central axis of Figure 5.4.

But arguably equal emphasis should be given to fidelity, flexibility and competence. One of the functions of the supervisor is to re-balance Figure 5.4 if necessary. This means that the supervisor needs to know the supervisee's training background and likely assumptive world. For example a volunteer counsellor partaking in an Introductory CBT Course may be mandated by the Charity not only to have CBT supervision but also Person Centred Supervision in relation to

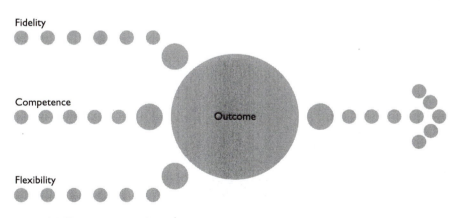

Figure 5.4 The active ingredients in treatment outcome.

clients treated with this modality; as such the notion of 'secondary gain' may be a readily available construct easily pressed into service. Whilst another supervisee may be a doctoral level psychologist with a belief that formulation is the centre-piece of cognitive therapy and that diagnosis constitutes an unnecessary labelling. The diversity of training backgrounds calls for considerable flexibility on the part of the supervisor, in ensuring that supervisees give equal weighting to each arm of Figure 5.4. It may well be, however, that different considerations apply in a low intensity intervention such as guided self-help (GSH). In GSH client contact is relatively brief and what might pass for an aspect of competence in traditional individual CBT, e.g. guided discovery, may lead the therapist to drift into a way of working that is more appropriate for high intensity work. Thus the focus in these comparatively brief interventions might be more appropriately on fidelity (adherence – specified treatment target and matching treatment strategy) and flexibility, e.g. adjusting reading material to the literacy level of the client, rather than trying fully to operationalise the construct of 'competence' in such a context.

Chapter 6

Specifying the problem

Supervisor, supervisee and client are each involved in collaborative problem solving. This chapter begins by highlighting the importance of problem definition, without which problem solving becomes fraught. But there can be alternative, equally valid definitions of a client's problem/s and in the next section the factors that go into clinical decision making in such real-world contexts are discussed. Service providers are accountable to their funding body and have typically justified their Service by reference to client outcomes on psychometric tests. But this is quite removed from multi-dimensional diagnostic assessments of randomised controlled trials and in the next section it is suggested that the one dimensional assessment is not fit for purpose, in that it does not clarify whether the identified problem/s have been resolved. Departures from an EBT can be justified by a supervisee, by an appeal to the 'complexity' of a particular client's difficulties, and in the next section it is suggested that this term may represent poor problem/s definition and consequent poorly focussed, non-evidence-based treatment. The next sections are concerned with how, paradoxically, an exclusive focus on client problems can lead to a missing of problems. In the penultimate section of this chapter it is suggested that part of the supervisor's role is to ensure that the supervisee develops a nuanced approach as to what is typically achieved with CBT for different disorders rather than that the latter is encouraged to become an evangelist for CBT. In the final section there is a discussion of how the supervisor can alert the supervisee to the operation of misleading stereotypes in the conduct of treatment.

Agreeing a definition of the problem

Unless a problem is precisely defined it cannot be solved. Imagine a client presenting with an opening gambit, such as '7-year-old Jack is just a pain, like his father'. One might gather from this that the client is not too enamoured of her son or his Dad. But it is not clear, who is doing what, when? The therapist might seek further clarification by using say the Eyberg Child Behavior Inventory (Eyberg and Ross, 1978) on which the parent indicates the frequency of 36 child behaviours and whether these are considered a problem or not. It might emerge from this, that the main problems are to do with child non-compliance, rather than say with stealing and lying, and therapeutic targets are thereby agreed. As a consequence the parent might be invited to attend a Group Parent Training Programme (see Scott and Stradling, 1987) However, the perception of child behaviour problems has been found to relate to a parent's emotional state (Najman *et al.*, 2000) and an alternative strategy might be to target this. The precision in the description of the parent's emotional state has, however, to match the precision with which the child behaviour problems are specified. For example it would be important to know whether the parent's depressed mood is part of the depressive phase of bipolar disorder or simply a major depressive disorder. In the latter case the parent might be offered individual or group cognitive therapy for depression. Thus the behavioural and diagnostic descriptions of a client's problems are complementary and may suggest different Evidence Based Treatments. EBTs are each tied to a clear specification of a problem.

Treatment decisions at the coalface

Clinical decision making is involved in the choice between EBTs, and which definition of the problem to lock onto: see Figure 6.1.

This is also informed by the client's preferences, for example, an individual or group intervention and by the expertise of the supervisee and supervisor, for example, whether one or other is adept at a group modality.

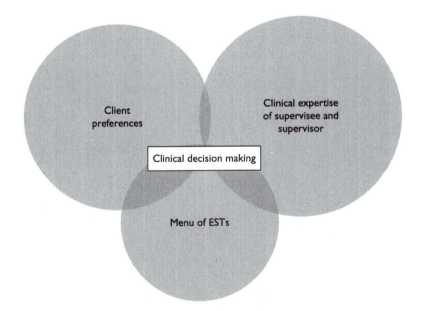

Figure 6.1 Clinical decision making and problem solving.

Whilst there is almost universal agreement that clinical expertise is important, the expertise of the engineers is rarely recognised. In conferences and journals for academic clinicians, 'Scientists' predominate and there is largely one-way traffic leading to a gulf between researchers and the synthesisers of research. In order to help remedy this situation Kazdin (2008) has suggested that those on the ground should codify their experience in such a manner that it becomes an archive on which others can draw. He is not suggesting that the Engineers analyse and publish their data in the way researchers do but rather that there is a distillation of accumulated wisdom. Arguably one of the functions of a supervisor should be to help the supervisee in the codification of their experiences, and the following example illustrates this:

SUPERVISEE: Sometimes I use trauma-focussed CBT and sometimes EMDR.

SUPERVISOR: Yes they are both NICE approved ESTs for PTSD, but how do you choose which to use with whom?

SUPERVISEE: I don't know really, I think if there is a bit of resistance when I suggest say writing about their trauma I go down the EMDR route.

SUPERVISOR: Is there any evidence that that is more acceptable?

SUPERVISEE: Not that I know of.

SUPERVISOR: If you compared the attendance records of the last dozen people you treated with EMDR and the last dozen people you treated with trauma-focussed CBT that would be interesting.

SUPERVISEE: But even if the attendance pattern turned out to have been the same I could still think I only made the attendance pattern of the EMDR clients as good by selecting them.

SUPERVISOR: That would be a possibility, but it could also be the case that selection makes no difference and with new clients you could look at what happens when you do no selection.

In this exchange the supervisor has helped the supervisee codify their past experience but also helped distil a framework for the codification of future work and both might be useful to the wider community of engineers. But this 'engineering' approach should not mean a non-recognition of the supervisee's emotional reaction in interviews; that too is data, as the following dialogue illustrates:

SUPERVISEE: As soon as I get PTSD clients to talk about their trauma they get upset and invariably say 'I don't like to talk about it', and I get a sinking feeling, because one way or another we are going to have to talk about it whether in trauma-focussed CBT or in EMDR.

SUPERVISOR: Sometimes pain is necessary, for example if you have back trouble and are put on traction there is more pain to begin with and that can be one way of justifying it.

SUPERVISEE: Yes.

SUPERVISOR: From your tone I sense a Yes . . . but.

SUPERVISEE: Hmm, but can't we somehow do better than this, with what amounts to head-on confrontation with a client.
SUPERVISOR: Maybe we should both look into this.
SUPERVISEE: Ok.

In this exchange the supervisor has given the supervisee space to express his/her feelings and they have been validated by a commitment to collaboratively seek a different way forward. The dialogue continues:

SUPERVISOR: I was looking at *CBT for Common Trauma Responses* (Scott (2012)) and he refers to some evidence for a non-trauma-focussed CBT, in which rather than initially focus on the trauma, you teach the client first what to say to themselves in preparation for a flashback, what to say to themselves when they encounter a flashback, what to say to themselves when feeling overwhelmed by it and the type of things they could say to themselves when they reflect on how their coping strategies are working.
SUPERVISEE: That sounds good.
SUPERVISOR: You could compare attendances for non-trauma-focussed CBT, trauma-focussed CBT and EMDR.
SUPERVISEE: Yes, it would be good to get organised for that.
SUPERVISOR: The only reference I could find on attendances was a Tarrier (2001) study of trauma-focussed CBT where on average clients attended every other session.

This dialogue illustrates how the various strands of Figure 6.1 are integrated in supervision. There can, however, be practical problems in the use of archival data and the collection of data, in terms of the clients' permission, but provided the data is suitably anonymous this should not present difficulties of publication in a journal but sometimes does, disadvantaging engineers. Whilst historically, there are a few journals that would claim to be open to what engineers might produce, for example *The Cognitive Behaviour Therapist*, *Behavioural and Cognitive Psychotherapy* (journals.cambridge.orbg/cbt) and *Cognitive and Behavioral Practice*, historically most of the authors have been academic clinicians, which is not particularly encouraging for most supervisors and supervisees.

One of the essentials of communicating a body of knowledge is a common language and in the sample dialogue above, both parties were clear that they were talking about clients with a specific disorder, PTSD, and because of this the exchange facilitates the supervisee's acquisition of competences required to conduct a first interview.

The need for a multi-dimensional assessment

In randomised controlled trials care is taken to ensure that any improvement in client functioning can be solely attributed to the intervention, and not to the passage of time. It is known, from naturalistic studies that, for example 54 per cent of those with depression recover within six months (Keller *et al.*, 1992), thus if a non-treatment sample of depressed clients were administered a psychometric test at two points in time one would expect a noticeable improvement in scores. Supervisors need to be aware of these methodological considerations in order to locate the practice of the supervisee in an evidence-based framework, as the following exchange illustrates:

SUPERVISEE: In our low intensity service we have just been evaluating our six-week group programme for depression. The results are good: an average score of 17 on the PHQ9 (a measure of the severity of depression (Kroenke *et al.*, 2001)) before and 10 after.

SUPERVISOR: How do you know that they would not have got better anyway?

SUPERVISEE: Well we compared the results to the results we got on the dropouts and they were more or less constant.

SUPERVISOR: Well they are likely to be for the very short period you had data on them.

SUPERVISEE: Well we have even got a lady who has done so well in the group, that she has come back as a co-leader to share her experience.

SUPERVISOR: I am sure she would be a very credible course of persuasion in the group, but what percentage of clients improved to the point that they were would no longer be regarded by themselves and others as suffering from depression?

SUPERVISEE: She fits the bill but I don't know the proportion.

SUPERVISOR: The danger is that in this situation you use the availability heuristic, the vivid positive experience of this client, to confirm your impression from the graph of on average decreasing scores as the programme progressed.

SUPERVISEE: I suppose you need the percentage improved in the group to the percentage that would have improved naturally.

SUPERVISOR: That would be a good start.

SUPERVISEE: Why only a start?

SUPERVISOR: Well I understand that one-third of people dropped out of the programme. When calculating the percentage recovered it will need to be based on all the people who came to at least one session and the figure will not be as good as when you look at the proportion of completers who recovered.

In this exchange the supervisor is educating the supervisee about the height of the bar a treatment has to jump over to be regarded as an Evidence Supported Treatment and that these concerns are germane to everyday practice and not the preserve of researchers. The dialogue continued:

SUPERVISEE: What is recovered anyway?

SUPERVISOR: I guess it is when the person is no longer affected by what they sought help for and when others would agree that they are no longer affected.

SUPERVISEE: My guess is that most people we see in our Programme would, at the end, still say that they are a little affected.

SUPERVISOR: It would useful to know how many would say they are no longer affected. How many would say that they are still a little affected? How many affected quite a lot? And how many are as bad or worse than they were when they first came to the Service? The Client Satisfaction Questionnaire (CSQ) (Attkisson and Zwick, R., 1982) I will just find it . . . yes Question 6 on the CSQ reads:

SUPERVISEE: It would give a clearer picture of what the Service is achieving.

SUPERVISOR: If you do the assessment of outcome from more than one dimension you get a better picture of what is going on. A self-report measure such as PHQ9 is one dimension, a satisfaction questionnaire such as the CSQ is another dimension. But questionnaires do have problems, clients can take an idiosyncratic view of a question, they can want to convey that they are really unwell so they tick the most extreme score on each question, they can want to feel that they have not wasted their or your time in attending a programme so indicate 'a little better'. There is a need for a third dimension in which in an interview you tease out how they are functioning in a standardised way; this makes it possible to compare the results with those in randomised controlled trials. It is admittedly time consuming but you have then got a 3-D picture of how the client has fared.

In the above dialogue the supervisor has highlighted the strengths and shortcomings of using self-report measures and the need for them to be complemented by the results of a standardised interview. The exchange continues:

SUPERVISEE: I don't know that I've got the time to do a diagnostic interview.

SUPERVISOR: But you do give the client space to explain their difficulties?

SUPERVISEE: Oh yes.

SUPERVISOR: How reliable is that interview?

SUPERVISEE: How do you mean?

SUPERVISOR: If ten other therapists were asking the same type of questions you ask, what would be the level of agreement in their conclusions?

SUPERVISEE: I guess it would be pretty mixed.

SUPERVISOR: Beck et al. (1962) in his original work found levels of agreement from such interviews of 32–54 per cent and this led to the development of standardised diagnostic interviews so that you could have a more solid base for planning interventions.

SUPERVISEE: As part of my job I have to spend an afternoon a week doing half hour telephone screen assessments.

SUPERVISOR: You may be stuck with that organisationally, but where is the evidence that it is reliable or indeed valid, i.e. leads to an intervention that is better than if a different conclusion had been arrived at?

SUPERVISEE: It is just tradition. But I suppose outside of the telephone assessments, I could use the *CBT Pocketbook* (Scott, 2009), which supplies diagnostic questions about each of the symptoms of a disorder, for cases that I may take on individually.

SUPERVISOR: There was a 'suppose' about asking diagnostic questions, sounds like there's a reservation.

SUPERVISEE: The clients will find such questions 'mechanical'.

SUPERVISOR: Have you used standardised diagnostic questions?

SUPERVISEE: Well no.

SUPERVISOR: How do you know they will find them 'mechanical'?

SUPERVISEE: Hmm, it would be a behavioural experiment?

SUPERVISOR: My hypothesis is that clients will feel that their world is more understood by such questions, but don't take my word for it, in the spirit of collaborative empiricism test it out.

SUPERVISEE: OK.

In the above dialogue the supervisor recognises common reservations about diagnostic interviews and addresses these concerns by reference to a behavioural experiment rather than insisting didactically that the supervisee engage in such an assessment. An alternative or complementary approach would have been to refer to the study of Bruchmuller, Margraf, Suppiger and Schneider (2011). These authors compared clients' views of the structured interview they had undergone, with therapists' estimates of the likely acceptance of such an assessment by clients. On a scale from 0 (not at all satisfied) to 100 (totally satisfied) clients rated overall satisfaction with a structured interview at $M = 86.55$. But therapists estimated significantly lower client acceptance $M = 49.41$, and this underestimation of acceptability is reflected in their finding that on average therapists use structured interviews with only 15 per cent of their clients. The above exchange also highlights the tension between the supervisee doing what is clinically necessary and what is economically viable. Ultimately, health economists are guided by what clinicians in power within an Organisation define as a good outcome, rather than by what clinicians without a vested interest may define as a good outcome. The exchange continues:

SUPERVISEE: So the 'gold standard' would be, that if, on the basis of a standardised interview using diagnostic criteria, a client was no longer clinically depressed, that would be good evidence of an impact.

SUPERVISOR: Well of all the dimensions you might assess, it is the most reliable. That is not to say that other dimensions would not flesh out the picture.

The intent of the supervisor is that the supervisee is encouraged to perform a rigorous assessment and this may or may not conform to the dictates of their Employer who has a vested interest in justifying the modus operandi, which can potentially skew the rigour of the assessment process. To a degree, supervision may have a subversive function as far as the Organisation is concerned, which can be potentially problematic if the latter funds the supervisor. From April 2013 NHS Hospitals have to use a 'Friends and Family Test' in which staff are asked whether they would recommend their Unit's service to a friend or relative based on the treatment delivered, and such a question would broaden the assessment of front-line mental health services.

Complexity?

Clients by definition present a challenge to the therapist, and there is an ever present danger of the supervisee/therapist short circuiting the assessment process by homing in on one problematic aspect of the client's functioning and on this basis labelling the client as 'complex', resulting in an inappropriate lowering of expectations. The following example illustrates this:

SUPERVISEE: John has PTSD and he drinks more than he should in the week when he does not have his kids to stay.
SUPERVISOR: Is he still going to work?
SUPERVISEE: Yes, he has the odd day off.
SUPERVISOR: What is the problem?
SUPERVISEE: He's complex, our cases are more complex than those in the trials.
SUPERVISOR: How do you know that?
SUPERVISEE: Well clients are specially selected in ESTs.
SUPERVISOR: The PTSD trials include clients with substance abuse although they exclude those with dependence. If it were the case that clients were that specially selected in ESTs then those studies are not relevant to routine practice, in what sense then could anyone be said to provide an EST?
SUPERVISEE: I need to look a bit more carefully at the notion of 'complexity'.

Whilst an overuse of the construct of complexity can lead to a lowering of expectations, it could also lead to the supervisee disengaging from a case as 'inappropriate'. In this dialogue the supervisor suggests that evidence based practice must have a link to ESTs to be credible. An understanding of the results of RCTs creates an upper bound as to what may be achieved in routine practice. RCTs do, however, typically exclude patients with a comorbid psychosis and those who are substance dependent or actively suicidal, to the extent that these features are present. Translation from the research context to routine practice is problematic.

Missing the problem

Use of a traditional open ended mental health interview has been found to result in missed diagnosis. In a study by Miller (2002) of inpatients fewer than half of write ups listed enough symptom criteria (e.g. hallucinations, depression) to meet DSM IV requirements for a diagnosis. This highlights a concern expressed by

Beck *et al.* (1962) that the traditional open interview does not control for information variance, i.e. the range of information that needs to be considered in making a diagnosis. Beck *et al.* (1962) also pointed out that the traditional open-ended interview also fails to control for criterion variance, i.e. the level at which a symptom has to be present to be regarded as clinically significant. Structured interviews control for both information and criterion variance, resulting in levels of agreement of 80–90 per cent.

Open-ended interviews tend to miss the presence of additional disorders (co-morbidity). In a study (Zimmerman and Mattia, 1999) comparing the prevalence of disorders in 500 clients given a traditional open-ended diagnostic interview, with 500 patients given a structured interview (SCID First *et al.* 1997), individuals interviewed with the SCID were assigned significantly more axis I diagnoses than individuals assessed with an unstructured interview. More than one-third of the clients interviewed with the SCID were diagnosed with three or more disorders, in contrast to fewer than 10 per cent of the clients assessed with an unstructured interview. Fifteen disorders were more frequently diagnosed in the SCID sample, and these differences occurred across mood, anxiety, eating, somatoform, and impulse-control disorder categories. The results suggest that in routine clinical practice, clinicians under-recognize diagnostic comorbidity. Anxiety, somatoform, and not otherwise specified (NOS) disorders were the most frequently under-detected disorders. This research was subsequently independently replicated in other settings (Basco *et al.*, 2000; Shear *et al.*, 2000; Miller *et al.*, 2002). In a study of 145 non-psychotic clients attending community clinics, Shear *et al.* (2000) found that 58 had been diagnosed as having an adjustment disorder using routine open-ended psychiatric interview, but by contrast when the 'gold standard', SCID (First *et al.*, 1997) interview was used only five met criteria for an adjustment disorder. (The SCID asks one or more questions about each symptom that comprises a disorder and specifies criteria for judging whether that symptom is present at a clinically significant level.) In addition, the SCID identified 22 sufferers from PTSD whilst the routine interview identified only one.

Further, there is evidence that using an open-ended interview clinicians tend to stop at the first disorder identified (Zimmerman and Mattia, 2000). This can have serious consequences, for example Panagioti, Gooding and Tarrier (2012) found that the suicidality of PTSD clients was strongly mediated by the level of comorbid depression. Thus a clinician using an open-ended interview with a traumatised client might readily identify what the clinician takes to be cardinal symptoms of PTSD e.g. nightmares/flashbacks but then neglect to make a sufficiently detailed enquiry about depression and thereby make a poor risk assessment. A structured interview ensures that no disorders are missed.

Diagnostic systems DSM IV and ICD 10 each utilise multi-axial classification systems that include axes specifying not only disorders such as depression, panic disorder, etc. but axes that document psychosocial and environmental problems, such as whether a client is having housing or economic problems or problems with his/her primary support group as well as an axis that indicates the overall level of functional impairment. In DSM IV and ICD 10 diagnosis is always located in a context and is not intended as a stand-alone total definition of the client's problem.

'All you need is to specify the client's problem'?

Few would doubt the importance of a specification of the client's problem/s, but there is no evidence that a psychosocial/environmental descriptor by itself leads to an EST. Whilst problem assessment is a legitimate focus in CBT courses it should be regarded as necessary but insufficient to usher in appropriate treatment. The following exchange illustrates this:

SUPERVISEE: I've had ten sessions with Liam, we made a good start and he responded to activity scheduling but he is back depressed. He separated from his wife last year, they had been married a year, stopped his cycling and had concentration problems at work. Basic problem is he has not been doing what he enjoys.

SUPERVISOR: Is that all or part of the problem?

SUPERVISEE: Well the depression and inactivity go hand-in-hand. I checked the depression with the DSM IV criteria and we have a good therapeutic alliance.

SUPERVISOR: A good therapeutic alliance?

SUPERVISEE: We agreed on the goal, to lift his depression, and the task to achieve this was to increase his activity and challenge his exaggeratedly negative thoughts and this has happened in the context of a good therapeutic relationship, lots of banter.

SUPERVISOR: All the key elements of the therapeutic alliance: goals, tasks and relationship are there. How would you explain the lack of success?

SUPERVISEE: I don't know.

SUPERVISOR: Is your problem your expectation of what a therapeutic alliance can achieve?

SUPERVISEE: It was a major focus on our course.

SUPERVISOR: Did you discuss its limitations?

SUPERVISEE: No, just got feedback on recordings as to how to improve the alliance.

SUPERVISOR: I suggest you read the Safran and Muan (2006) paper on it and we could talk about it next time.

The above dialogue highlights the often uncritical emphasis on the therapeutic alliance in CBT training courses, leading to a simplistic focus on goals, tasks and the therapeutic relationship. In fact the paper by Safran and Muran (2006) reveals that the therapeutic alliance only accounts for 6 per cent of outcome. The exchange continued at the next session:

SUPERVISEE: Why such an emphasis on the alliance in courses when it has so little effect?

SUPERVISOR: You tell me.

SUPERVISEE: I suppose it simplifies matters for teachers and students.

SUPERVISOR: It may also be acceptable because it strikes a balance between the task orientation of CBT and the relationship aspects that are given more emphasis in humanistic and psychodynamic therapies.

SUPERVISEE: But actually it is not a lot of use.

SUPERVISOR: Not a lot; arguably it functions more as a heuristic and can distract from other things like a comprehensive assessment.

SUPERVISEE: How do you mean?

SUPERVISOR: Well when you got stuck with Liam, probably the most important thing would be to do a re-assessment, go through again the predisposing factors, the precipitants and maintaining factors – no one was there for him, he buried himself in school work, no real friends until he met the person who was to become his wife.

SUPERVISOR: What happened in the marriage?

SUPERVISEE: If she criticised him he went into a sulk, then withdrew; she would become angry and accuse him of not confiding.

SUPERVISOR: He might be depressed but this could be a spin-off of an avoidant personality disorder, and you may need to assess for this as it is a different treatment than depression; you could look at *Beck's Cognitive Therapy of Personality Disorder* (Beck, Freeman and Davis, 2007).

SUPERVISEE: I'll get hold of that, but I'm concerned about what we are saying about the therapeutic alliance, it's not what most would say.

SUPERVISOR: I wouldn't deny that the relationship is important in CBT; without it the technical aspects would be wasted. But beyond gauging whether a therapist has the empathy, warmth and genuineness to deliver the technical aspects, there is at best a minimal return for the added attention to the relationship. Historically in CBT outcome studies of DSM IV axis one disorders, such as depression, anxiety, OCD, attention to the relationship has been no more than I have suggested should be the case. But interestingly in CBT for personality disorders (Axis II in DSM IV American Psychiatric Association (2000)) there is more of an emphasis on the relationship.

SUPERVISEE: Does CBT for personality disorders work?

SUPERVISOR: Compared to CBT for Axis 1 disorders?

SUPERVISEE: Yes.

SUPERVISOR: Have a look at the literature and see what you think.

The above dialogue illustrates that having a mult-axial classification system for clients increases the range of possible therapeutic interventions and can illuminate a supervisee's 'stuck points'. Supervision is by definition hierarchical and the supervisor must express his/her opinion; in this respect CBT supervision differs from supervision in humanistic or psychodynamic therapy. Without such openness there would be a poor relationship between supervisor and supervisee. Nevertheless the supervisor has taken care not to impose his/her opinion on matters. The supervisor has acknowledged that there is a range of opinion in CBT about the importance of the relationship with the client but in the spirit of collaborative empiricism suggests the supervisee assesses the evidence for this differential emphasis themselves.

SUPERVISEE: Liam is a perfect match for the DSM IV criteria for avoidant personality disorder (American Psychiatric Association, 2000). I found a paper by Emmelkamp and colleagues (2006) comparing CBT with brief dynamic therapy (BDT) for avoidant personality disorder. The CBT Manual used was Beck and Freeman's (1990) book. At follow up 9 per cent of those undergoing CBT still met DSM IV criteria for avoidant personality disorder while 36 per cent of those who had BDT no longer met criteria. Clients in BDT did no better than those on a waiting list.

SUPERVISOR: That's good but I don't know of any other randomised controlled trial for avoidant personality disorder.

SUPERVISEE: So using the Chambless and Hollon (1998) criteria (Appendix C) CBT would only be regarded as 'possibly efficacious' as opposed to 'efficacious'.

SUPERVISOR: Yes, it is a 'definite maybe'; it is not known whether a more traditional CBT would have been just as effective.

In this dialogue the supervisor has modelled an openness to new developments in the delivery of CBT but within a critical awareness of what constitutes evidence in outcome studies. The next section addresses the education of the supervisee on what may constitute change in clients.

Distilling an appropriate yardstick

The following exchange shows that an appreciation of the specifics of outcome studies can encourage the supervisee, circumventing striving for an unattainable therapeutic ideal:

SUPERVISEE: I guess looking at the results of an EST would be a stringent test of how we are doing.

SUPERVISOR: Strangely it might also provide some comfort, as by no means everybody in an EST recovers.

SUPERVISEE: I thought it was about 80 per cent.

SUPERVISOR: What made you think that?

SUPERVISEE: It's what I picked up at a workshop.

SUPERVISOR: It may be that the researchers were citing a particular study that achieved 80 per cent recovery; whilst that might have been achieved for some panic disorder protocols, I can't think of any other disorder where 4 out of 5 recover. Maybe the vividness of the experience has led you to overgeneralise about these results, perhaps you are operating with an availability heuristic in forming a judgment about the standard of therapeutic intervention to be achieved?

SUPERVISEE: I can see the importance of realistic expectations.

Table 6.1 Mean percentage improved

	Depression	Panic disorder	Generalised anxiety disorder
Completers	51%	63%	52%
Intention to treat	37%	54%	44%

Source: Westen and Morrison (2001)

In this exchange the supervisor has been concerned to ensure not only that the supervisee is rigorously assessing the outcome of interventions but with empowering the latter by constructing a more realistic view of what is achievable. As such the scientific and humanitarian concerns dovetail. The dialogue continues as the supervisor clarifies what is achieved in ESTs:

SUPERVISOR: Table 6.1 shows the mean percentage improved across studies for depression, panic disorder and generalised anxiety disorder in Westen and Morrison's meta-analysis (2001).

Of those that complete treatment roughly half improve, but if you include dropouts, the bottom row of Table 6.1, the percentage of improvers is slightly less than half.

SUPERVISEE: Good, but not wonderful.
SUPERVISOR: Yes; in the same study, Westen and Morrison (2001) showed for example that the average client undergoing treatment for panic disorder had just less than one (0.7) panic attacks a week and endorsed 4 of the possible 17 symptoms of panic disorder, i.e. they would be regarded as still having limited symptom panic attacks
SUPERVISEE: It gives me some realistic expectations with regards to these clients.
SUPERVISOR: The results mean that there has to be a continued openness to treatments that might do better, but there has to be rigorous analysis as to whether they constitute added value.
SUPERVISEE: But in routine practice you would treat a client with limited symptom panic attacks.
SUPERVISOR: That is where you have to take great care in interpreting the findings of Table 6.1. They all refer to clients with DSM IV defined depression, panic disorder and GAD; they are not a reliable guide if you are including clients with subclinical levels of disorders. It may well be that CBT is particularly efficacious with clients with a subclinical level of disorders, but we simply don't know because the research has not been conducted.
SUPERVISEE: If you don't know exactly what the client is suffering from then you can't have a yardstick.
SUPERVISOR: That's the problem with some of the studies conducted in routine practice such as Westbrook and Kirk (2005) and Brown *et al.* (2011) which

involved no standardised diagnostic interview, relying instead on self-report measures; they are not a useful metric.

This dialogue illustrates once again that diagnosis provides a common language not only for understanding the results of ESTs but also for defining the upper limit of what might be obtained in routine practice with a client from the same client population. This is not to say that diagnosis is the only yardstick for identifying a population. In the following exchange the supervisee is a member of an Early Intervention for Psychosis Team and the focus of discussion in supervision is on preventative work:

SUPERVISEE: Our team is beginning to look at CBT for preventing transition to psychosis in an at-risk group.
SUPERVISOR: Sounds great, but how realistic is this?
SUPERVISEE: A study by Morrison *et al.* (2012) found that giving CBT to an at-risk group meant only 8 per cent made the transition to psychosis.
SUPERVISOR: What is the usual rate of transition?
SUPERVISEE: There seems to be some debate on this but my understanding is that it was at least twice as high.
SUPERVISOR: How was an at-risk group defined?
SUPERVISEE: I know the average age was 20, but I'm not sure how they were selected.
SUPERVISOR: You would need the same selection procedure for the same results.
SUPERVISEE: Yes, I'll look at how they defined at risk.

In the sample dialogue, the focus is on defining the target population so that results from an EST might be translated to routine practice but, as the continuing exchange indicates, the descriptors do not have to be confined to a diagnosis:

SUPERVISEE: It seems that the 'at-risk' group fall under a number of headings: those with either transient psychotic symptoms or subclinical psychotic symptoms or diminished functioning together with a first degree relative with a history of psychosis or a pre-existing schizotypal personality disorder.
SUPERVISOR: That sounds like a pretty vulnerable population, and I can see that a yardstick you might use is avoiding transition to psychosis, but avoiding transition to other disorders such as depression might also be an important yardstick athough it is not one addressed in the Morrison *et al.* (2012) study.
SUPERVISEE: One of the treatment targets in the CBT provided was depression and treatment was according to a manual.
SUPERVISOR: Yes, I gather there were weekly supervision sessions and monthly peer supervision sessions to ensure fidelity to the manual.

This dialogue illustrates that even when an intervention is not diagnosis specific there is a need to specify the problem carefully and manualise the treatment approach so that it can be replicated by others in other settings.

Misleading stereotypes

'He looks evil, he must be evil': a person believing this is most likely operating on a stereotype of a scarred, somewhat ugly, male and the unfortunate person under inspection is seen as a match to the prototype. One would expect almost all therapists to be able to step around this non sequitur but therapists are not free of their own stereotypes which in turn can lead to a misspecification of the problem. In a study of the accuracy of a diagnosis of agoraphobia by Schmidt *et al.* (2005) therapists were asked to rate hypothetical clients with symptom profiles emphasising one or other of the three sufficient criteria (avoidance, use of companions or endurance of situations despite distress). In fact therapists weighted the criteria differently. Avoidance was most likely to produce a diagnosis, even if according to DSM IV, each of the three criteria is equally sufficient for a diagnosis. This shows that clinical diagnosis is also affected by heuristic reasoning. To take a further example, it is known that ADHD is more common in boys than girls, a ratio of 3:1, but in routine practice the ratio is 6–9:1. Bruchmuller *et al.* (2012) have demonstrated that therapists use the representativeness heuristic and assign a diagnosis on the basis of whether the person before them resembles their concept of a prototypical ADHD child, leading to overdiagnosis of ADHD. Bruchmuller *et al.* (2012: 137) concluded

> one way to reduce the influence of diagnostic biases would be to establish more compulsory and thorough diagnostic training of prospective therapists. Only if therapists recognise how easily diagnostic decisions can be biased can they avoid such pitfalls. In addition, our results indicate how important it is to use structured interviews and other standardized tools as accepted instruments in clinical practice.

These may have added that it should be mandatory for supervisors to ensure that their supervisees engage in rigorous assessment.

Chapter 7

Adherence

Professional incompetence is rightly the subject of censure and sometimes the focus of litigation. Competence refers to the skills with which a procedure/intervention is conducted. But incompetence invariably begins with a departure from accepted/evidence-based treatment. Competence is rather like a magnificent house but it is erected on a foundation of treatment adherence – it is predicated on a knowledge of what to do with whom, and unless the foundation is solid the superstructure crumbles. For example an Orthopaedic Surgeon's competence in practising keyhole surgery depends first of all on adhering to a protocol in identifying suitable cases. It is possible to perform effectively using formulation driven CBT, but it is rather like going fishing without a rod; you may catch something but it is much easier with the rod (a knowledge of diagnostic specific procedures). This chapter begins with suggestions as to how treatment adherence may be addressed. The codification of treatment adherence can of course be jettisoned by a wholly individualistic formulation driven treatment and the case for this is examined in the following section. In the final section it is suggested that without due consideration of treatment adherence the focus can easily shift to the irrelevant.

Assessing treatment adherence

Assessing whether something has been done (adherence) is always likely to be an easier task than assessing how well it has been done (competence) but in the CBT literature comparatively little attention has been paid to treatment adherence compared to competence. The following vignette illustrates the need for the dual assessment of adherence and competence:

SUPERVISOR: I watched the DVD of your session with Danielle and I read your background note on her.
SUPERVISEE: I thought that session went well.
SUPERVISOR: *Laughing* That's not why you gave it to me, is it?
SUPERVISEE: Of course not!
SUPERVISOR: I thought there was great rapport, and you were collaboratively working through her Thought Record. Danielle was clearly upset about her

parents dropping everything when her brother comes home from University and neglecting her, and you did a good piece of Socratic dialogue to help her appreciate that it was an arbitrary inference to conclude that she was a 'waste of space and didn't matter'.

SUPERVISEE: Yes, at the very end of the previous session she had commented that her brother was coming home for the holidays and she wasn't looking forward to it.

SUPERVISOR: I think you did well picking this up from one session and addressing it in the next; rather than talk about her low self-esteem in the abstract you focussed on her 'hot cognitions' about her brother to access these negative core beliefs. From a CBT skill point of view you did really well but it didn't quite fit with your note about Danielle.

SUPERVISEE: How do you mean?

SUPERVISOR: Well you said that she has OCD and sometimes gets depressed. If I had watched the DVD without the note my guess would have been this was a depressed client. When she came to treatment what was the main problem she was complaining about?

SUPERVISEE: OCD. I thought I had done well bridging from one session to another.

SUPERVISOR: You had; it was highly skilled but given that all the session was devoted to the Thought Record/ mood management were you delivering what was essentially being asked for?

SUPERVISEE: I think I would argue that I was adhering to a depression protocol.

SUPERVISOR: I take your point, certainly looking at the Adherence Scale for Depression, Table 7.1 (*reproduced in Appendix D*), you did well.

SUPERVISEE: Yes, I had that on my lap in the session as a guidance.

SUPERVISOR: But not the adherence scale for OCD as well?

SUPERVISEE: No.

SUPERVISOR: I wasn't clear from your note whether Danielle was assessed as being depressed.

SUPERVISEE: Well it's a bit of a grey area, she had just four DSM IV symptoms rather than the five or more required for a diagnosis.

SUPERVISOR: That probably does legitimate a focus on depressive symptoms, but there really ought to have been linkage to OCD symptoms. For example, did Danielle do more hand washing/cleaning when she was low?

SUPERVISEE: Yes, I've missed the bigger picture.

SUPERVISOR: What we could do is compare your ratings on the Treatment Adherence Scale for Depression with mine.

SUPERVISEE: OK, I don't think we had much discussion on depression about depression.

SUPERVISOR: I gave a two there as you at least tangentially addressed depression about depression, by normalising her response, disclosing that you felt irritated by your mother always telling people how well your older brother has done.

SUPERVISEE: I think a two is about right. I gave a three for inactivity as we discussed her not staying in her room when her brother comes home but going for walks, visiting friends.

Table 7.1 Treatment adherence scale: Depression

Treatment adherence: Depression

How thoroughly were specific treatment targets and techniques addressed in the session?:

1 Not done	2	3 Some discussion	4	5 Considerable discussion	6	7 Extensively discussed

Treatment target	Technique	Score
1. Depression about depression	Focus on responsibility for working on solutions and not on responsibility for problem	
2. Inactivity	Developing a broad investment portfolio, wide-ranging modest investments	
3. Negative views of self, personal world and future	Challenging the validity, utility and authority by which these views are held. Use of MOOD chart	
4. Information processing biases	Highlighting personal biases and stepping around them using MOOD chart	
5. Overvalued roles	Valuing multiple roles, renegotiation of roles in social context	
	Mean score	

SUPERVISOR: Yes, I think a three is what I would have scored you, and there was lots of discussion on items 3 and 4, I'd say they were 6 or 7.

SUPERVISEE: Well I thought they were at least a 5!

SUPERVISION: I thought there was a lot of focus on renegotiation of role. I liked your bit about not having auditioned for the role of Cinderella, worth a 7!

The Adherence Scales are derived from a format, used originally by Huppert *et al.* (2001) in the context of panic disorder, and integrated with the Sat Navs for depression and each of the anxiety disorders in Scott (2011). The set of Adherence Scales are presented in Appendix D. In the study by Huppert *et al.* (2001), involving 14 highly trained therapists, they had a mean score of 5.7 (s.d. 0.7) and perhaps because their scores clustered around the high end of the scale, their adherence scores did not predict outcome in panic disorder, but with a larger spread of scores to be expected in routine practice it may be expected that the Adherence Scale would be predictive. There are no norms on the derived Adherence Scales, at present they are simply an aid to practice and supervision. A different CBT treatment for a disorder, e.g. behavioural activation (see Martell, Dimidjian and Herman-Dunn, 2010) for depression, may require a somewhat different Adherence Scale. The supervision session continued:

SUPERVISOR: Looking at the Adherence Scale for OCD, Table 7.2 (*reproduced in Appendix D*), I suppose that you were tackling item 7, low mood, but not in relation to OCD.

SUPERVISEE: It is difficult to see how I could have scored more than 1s on anything but item 7.

SUPERVISOR: I agree, with regard to adherence a holistic approach is required interweaving protocols for each disorder and at the same time being compliant with each protocol.

SUPERVISEE: Looking back I should have made space for protocols for each disorder when I negotiated an agenda with Danielle at the start of the session.

SUPERVISOR: I think that is right.

The above vignette illustrates how use of the Adherence Scales can prevent therapeutic drift and refocus treatment. Whilst attending to the client's latest crisis can be an opportunity to focus on 'hot cognitions' it may not necessarily mean that the most salient cognitions are under scrutiny, and a balance may need to be struck between the two. Treatment adherence informs competence – fidelity to treatment protocols sets the scene for the exhibition of competences and they both presume an accurate assessment of the client's problem/s.

Jettisoning treatment adherence?

A number of authors including Persons (2006) and Grant, Townend, Mills and Cockx (2008) have contended that there are too many disorder specific protocols, with in some cases different ESTs for the same disorder, and that a clinician in routine practice would be overwhelmed by this bewildering array. Further they contend that clients in routine practice do not present with a single disorder as in controlled trials but have a number of disorders making diagnosis specific protocols impractical. Their solution to these alleged difficulties is a case-formulation driven CBT. This different perspective on treatment adherence can surface in supervision, and supervisor and supervisee may hold different positions resulting in potential conflict. The following exchange illustrates a way around this by an appeal to evidence-based treatment:

SUPERVISEE: I've used the Five Aspect case formulation (see Grant, Townend, Mills and Cockx, 2008) approach to get a picture of what is going on with Daksha. I've written the formulation down here (*handing it to supervisor*).

Table 7.2 Treatment adherence scale: Obsessive compulsive disorder

Treatment adherence: Obsessive compulsive disorder

How thoroughly were specific treatment targets and techniques addressed in the session?:

1	2	3	4	5	6	7
Not done		Some discussion		Considerable discussion		Extensively discussed

Treatment target	Technique	Score
1. Model of mental life, serious misinterpretation of intrusions thought action fusion (TAF), thought object fusion (TOF) and thought event fusion (TEF)	Develop more appropriate model, detached mindfulness about intrusions	
2. Inappropriate goal state, e.g. absolute certainty, perfect cleanliness	Distilling achievable goals	
3. Appraisal of intrusions	Encourage perception of reasonable degree of control by postponement strategies. Use of bOCD chart and completion of Personal Significance Scale	
4. Neutralising images, thoughts, behaviours	Behavioural experiments, Dare – Don't Avoid a Realistic Experiment	
5. Overestimation of danger/intolerance of uncertainty	Distillation of realistic probabilities. The necessity of tolerating uncertainty	
6. Cognitive and behavioural avoidance	Demonstration of the harmlessness of thoughts. Discussion of 'why don't you warn others of these dangers?'	
7. Excessive responsibility, low mood	Responsibility pie, therapist contracts to remove responsibility, MOOD chart, memory aids	
8. Unassertive communication	Communication guidelines	
9. Unrealistic appraisals of the personal significance of intrusions	Challenging appraisals, 'devil's advocate'	
Mean score		

SUPERVISOR: So under 'relevant history', you've got 'always put down by mum, always low self-esteem. Dad died when very young. Married at twenty to get away from Mum, marriage soon broke up and with new partner, Dilip, and she has two children with him aged four (Lina) and two (Ben). Lina is monitored by Hospital and Nursery and is on the at-risk register. Daksha has had panic attacks since Social Services involvement'. Under a heading 'environmental' you have put 'Social Service visits/meetings', under the heading 'physiological/biological' you put 'apprehension/tension', under the heading 'behavioural' you put ' makes herself scarce when they visit, leaves it to partner or gets into an argument with them', then under the heading 'emotional' you put 'very stressed by all this' and under the heading 'cognitive' you put 'believes she can't win if avoids the social worker, it's "suspicious" and if she sees them she is told she is "hostile"'. Finally under the heading 'Reinforcing life experiences' you put ' Daksha feels like it's the same as trying to have a sensible conversation with her own mother'. That gives a pretty clear picture of how Daksha is stressed on a day-to-day basis, what is your game plan with it?

SUPERVISEE: I think I've got to help Daksha work through the fact that the social worker isn't her mother and she is not as powerless as she thinks.

SUPERVISOR: I can see how you might go in that direction but the Five Aspect case formulation form also has a heading 'Diagnosis (DSM IV or ICD 10): (i)_____(ii)_____ why didn't you put anything there?

SUPERVISEE: It doesn't matter that much.

SUPERVISOR: Why is it there then?

SUPERVISEE: We never bothered much with that at College, I suppose you might put in depression and panic disorder.

SUPERVISOR: And what might that mean about the rest of the Five Aspects diagram?

SUPERVISEE: I don't know.

SUPERVISOR: What about the cognitive content disorder specificity hypothesis (Alford and Beck, 1997)?

SUPERVISEE: I've heard about that somewhere, jog my memory.

SUPERVISOR: That disorders are distinguished by their different cognitive content.

SUPERVISEE: I don't see how that fits into my picture.

SUPERVISOR: It doesn't seem to have played any role, what you have focussed on is the vivid drama played out between Daksha and Social Services, those problems are clearly indicated and I think everyone would agree that they are an issue, but what are the underlying cognitions?

SUPERVISEE: That the social worker will be as unrewarding as mum.

SUPERVISOR: What is the range of information pertinent to a formulation?

SUPERVISEE: You just test out your hypothesis, so that if I get Daksha to stick around long enough with the social worker she will collect experimental evidence that not everyone is like mum.

SUPERVISOR: But this is an arbitrary focus; you could argue that as 40 per cent of the social workers involved in Child Protection are unqualified, she may well find the experience unrewarding, to say the least, and it confirms her view of female authority figures.

SUPERVISEE: Hmm, I must admit I couldn't get a clear idea as to why Lina is on the at-risk register; her two-year-old brother is perfectly fine and mum is very small and of slight build anyway.

SUPERVISOR: What have the Hospital said about Lina?

SUPERVISEE: They haven't been able to say exactly why Lina isn't thriving; the Nursery picked up on some odd mannerisms initially such as rocking and wanting to sit on the lap of staff rather than play with other children.

SUPERVISOR: What we have just got into is a 'formulation', in which there could be a lot of competing theories which within the confines of therapy likely will not get us far; an alternative approach is a 'case formulation' approach.

SUPERVISEE: But this is real-world therapy away from the neat single disorder protocols of controlled trials, and what I see in routine practice doesn't match them.

In the above dialogue the training of the supervisee has led to an effective jettisoning of disorder specific protocols in favour of a formulation driven CBT that has a 'real-world feel'. Further RCTs are seen by the supervisee as being of doubtful relevance. The supervisor has endeavoured to point out that such formulations are fairly arbitrary and that the therapeutic pathways they suggest have few reliable landmarks. At the next supervision session the dialogue continues:

SUPERVISEE: Things have got worse with Daksha, she has put her daughter Lina into care because she is tired of being as she sees it 'pestered' by the social workers.

SUPERVISOR: So what have you been doing in the sessions?

SUPERVISEE: Just providing emotional support.

SUPERVISOR: What about the panic disorder and depression?

SUPERVISEE: It's been more crisis stuff.

SUPERVISOR: Going back to the formulation form in Grant, Townend, Mills and Cockx (2008) if you had concluded that she had suffered from panic disorder and depression and entered this on the form, this could have focussed attention on specific cognitions in relation to each disorder: for example catastrophic cognitions in relation to panic and depressogenic cognitions about possibly a loss of a valued role about being a mother.

SUPERVISEE: I see, the diagnosis suggests particular cognitions that could have been a target; as it is I've drifted into counselling haven't I?

SUPERVISOR: Looks like it, looking at the Treatment Adherence Scale for panic disorder, Appendix D would have highlighted the need to focus on catastrophic cognitions and looking at the Treatment Adherence Scale for depression (Table 7.1, reproduced in Appendix D) you may have looked at cognitions surrounding a loss of a valued role.

SUPERVISEE: I could have still usefully done that without denying the horror of the situation Daksha is in, but what I picked up from the course and the Grant, Townend, Mills and Cockx (2008) book was that diagnosis was very much an optional extra.

SUPERVISOR: Perhaps we ought to both look at this book before the next session?

SUPERVISEE: OK.

The above vignette shows that the protocols from controlled trials, enshrined in the Treatment Adherence Scales, are very relevant to the concerns that arise in routine practice. This echoes the findings of Stirman *et al.* (2005) that the characteristics of 80 per cent of clients in routine practice were such that they would have been admitted to one or more controlled trials. Further most RCTs allow a degree of comorbidity; for example most panic disorder and PTSD studies allow that the client may also suffer from depression but not to the point that it is the main disorder for which they are seeking treatment, as well as including those who abuse alcohol but exclude those who are dependent. It is a caricature of controlled trials to claim that the clients in these studies are not representative of those in routine practice. At the next supervision session the dialogue continued:

SUPERVISEE: I found the following quote in Grant, Townend, Mills and Cockx (2008: 20),

> We are, however less convinced of their value (*standardised diagnostic interviews*) within routine practice when an experienced cognitive behavioural psychotherapist is assessing a client. However, it can be argued that practice with a standardised interview can extremely valuable to a less experienced therapist or where the therapist is assessing a problem of which they have little or no previous experience.

SUPERVISOR: But when you were doing your course were you not 'less experienced'?

SUPERVISEE: I suppose so.

SUPERVISOR: So why wasn't the course encouraging you to use a standardised diagnostic interview?

SUPERVISEE: It doesn't look as if it was part of the zeitgeist.

SUPERVISOR: What is the empirical evidence that an experienced cognitive behavioural therapist can reliably conduct CBT without a standardised diagnostic interview?

SUPERVISEE: I don't know of any.

SUPERVISOR: Person (2006) has made a case for formulation driven CBT, but strangely in her study she assessed all clients using the DSM IV criteria and it cannot be assumed that these diagnostic conclusions did not inform the treatment meted out.

SUPERVISEE: I found it worrying to read in Grant, Townend, Mills and Cockx (2008: 66), 'in the absence of knowledge about the reliability and validity of case formulation, its use constitutes an act of faith on the part of both therapist and client – in our view a worthwhile one'.

SUPERVISOR: It appears that what those authors and Person (2006) are actually talking about is 'formulation' and not 'case formulation'. In Beck's original work a case formulation was simply a specific example of the cognitive model of a disorder. For example one person's catastrophic cognitions in panic disorder might be about having a heart attack whereas in another 'case' those catastrophic cognitions might be about making a show of themselves in front of others during a panic attack.

SUPERVISEE: But how do you juggle protocols for different disorders?

SUPERVISOR: What is the evidence that it is a 'juggle'?

SUPERVISEE: That seems to be what they say when they talk about a transdiagnostic approach.

SUPERVISOR: But what is the evidence that it is an unmanageable 'juggle'?

SUPERVISEE: I guess I should conduct a behavioural experiment and implement simultaneous protocols and see what happens.

SUPERVISOR: It is no different to having to manage a patient's diabetes whilst attending to their heart problems. Fundamentally we have no evidence that a formulation driven CBT performs comparably or better to following the prescriptions embedded in the RCTs.

This dialogue suggests that jettisoning treatment adherence is not evidence-based or dictated by the needs of routine practice. However, some skill is involved in interweaving the protocols for different disorders. The ways in which this is achieved are described in Scott (2009).

Focussing on the irrelevant

There is no limit to the range of information that might be considered pertinent to a purely formulation driven CBT and it is therefore easy for a therapist to resemble Don Quixote 'tilting at windmills'. The following vignette illustrates this:

SUPERVISEE: Daksha mentioned that when Lina was about two, just before her brother was born, the police raided their house, she heard a 'bang' and the next thing she knew armed officers were in her bedroom, and she and her partner were marched downstairs, Lina began screaming and after a few minutes she was allowed to collect her under supervision from her room, and they were all asked to stay in the living room, while the police searched the property. Daksha wanted to go to the toilet and they wouldn't let her, there was no female officer with them, she became distressed, they repeatedly asked her partner if he was someone he had never heard of, and he said 'no'. After about an hour the police established that the person they were looking for was a previous tenant, and they apologised and left. Daksha had difficulty sleeping after that and I wonder did it affect Lina?

SUPERVISOR: Could have affected the baby – it is very difficult to know with a child so young.

SUPERVISEE: I think I probably need to get Daksha to talk about it more.

SUPERVISOR: Does she have flashbacks of the incident?

SUPERVISEE: Don't think so.

SUPERVISOR: Does she have nightmares of the incident?

SUPERVISEE: Don't think so.

SUPERVISOR: What sort of screen did you use for such difficulties?

SUPERVISEE: I just used the Functional Analysis Assessment in Grant, Townend, Mills and Cockx (2008: 14–16).

SUPERVISOR: But that assessment interview did not pick up the police raid.

SUPERVISEE: No.

SUPERVISOR: How has that assessment interview screened for specific disorders?

SUPERVISEE: Well it has a 'Mental Status' section that refers to 'appearance, speech, mood, appetite, sleep, libido, anhedonia, irritability, self-worth and self-image, hopelessness, risk/self-harm/suicide, psychosis, concentration, orientation and memory'.

SUPERVISOR: They are all important areas to ask about, but what is the evidence that they are either a sufficient screen for a disorder or that a reliable diagnosis can be made on their basis?

SUPERVISEE: It's what I've seen most psychiatrists use in routine practice.

SUPERVISOR: But the reliability of such open-ended interviews covering those domains is between 32 and 54 per cent (Beck *et al.*, 1962), that is why they are not used in research and have been replaced by standardised interviews in which a question is asked about each symptom of a disorder.

SUPERVISEE: But I'm not doing research.

SUPERVISOR: No, but you could have used a standardised screen for each of the disorders; the one for PTSD is Table 7.3 (from the First Step Questionnaire, Scott (2011)).

A positive response to three of the symptom questions is an effective screen for PTSD, suggesting that further questioning about each of the PTSD symptoms is required.

SUPERVISEE: And the final question would have alerted me as to whether PTSD symptoms are an issue for her or not.

SUPERVISOR: Yes, if Daksha is depressed, which is quite likely given all that is going on with her daughter, she will tend to ruminate on anything that has gone wrong in the past, but that doesn't mean those incidents are a problem per se.

SUPERVISEE: Hmm, could have stopped me focussing on the irrelevant.

Table 7.3 Screen for PTSD

Post-traumatic stress disorder	Yes	No	Don't know
In your life, have you ever had any experience that was so frightening, horrible or upsetting that, in the past month, you:			
i. Have had nightmares about it or thought about it when you did not want to?			
ii. Tried hard not to think about it or went out of your way to avoid situations that reminded you of it?			
iii. Were constantly on guard, watchful, or easily startled?			
iv. Felt numb or detached from others, activities, or your surroundings?			
Is this something with which you would like help?			

SUPERVISOR: Certainly it would have highlighted what was important or not important for Daksha. Is there perhaps something around drinking or substance abuse that has got Social Services worried?

SUPERVISEE: I don't think so. As part of my assessment I asked how many units of alcohol she consumes a week, and it translated to about 14 units a week, which is about OK.

SUPERVISOR: But if you had used a standardised screen for alcohol/drugs (Table 7.4 from the First Step Questionnaire Scott (2011)) you would have had a clearer picture. Positive response to at least two of the symptom questions would suggest that the alcohol use needs more detailed enquiry and you would have picked up from the 'help' question whether this was an issue that she wanted help for.

SUPERVISEE: The 'help' question is an interesting one because it allows the client to be ambivalent about an issue, and that is important to know from a therapeutic point of view. I notice that in the First Step Questionnaire/ 7-Minute Interview the 'help' question is attached to each screen for each disorder.

There is some evidence that a client's readiness to adopt change strategies appears to predict the speed with which depressive symptoms resolve in CBT clients with depression and the anxiety disorders (Lewis, Simons and Kim, 2012). Those who were more contemplative, i.e. seeing advantages and disadvantages in changing their behaviour, were more likely to speedily reduce their depressive symptoms than those who were pre-contemplative, i.e. they do not recognise their difficulty as a problem that they needed to address. The First Step Questionnaire and its

Table 7.4 Screen for substance abuse/dependence

Substance abuse/dependence	Yes	No	Don't know
i. Have you felt guilty about your drinking/drug use?			
ii Have you felt you should cut down on your alcohol/drug?			
iii. Have people got annoyed with you about your drinking/drug taking?			
iv. Do you drink/use drugs before midday?			
Is this something with which you would like help?			

interview counterpart The 7-Minute Interview provide an indication of how contemplative/pre-contemplative the client is and this can be a useful therapeutic focus. This is exemplified in the following exchange in a supervision session:

SUPERVISEE: I find Margaret really frustrating. She was referred for depression. The depression is, I think, severe, and when I asked her whether she had thoughts of hurting herself she said 'I don't think I will ever do it because I've never done it, but I think of putting my tablets in a bottle of water and taking it on a long train journey, I don't want to be a trouble to anyone with anything dramatic'.

SUPERVISOR: Hmm, worrying. There don't seem to be any reasons for living?

SUPERVISEE: No, usually you get people saying they wouldn't do it because of their children or parents.

SUPERVISOR: There may be something in what she is saying in that those who have made previous parasuicide attempts are more likely to make further attempts. Does she drink or is she impulsive?

SUPERVISEE: No.

SUPERVISOR: I guess she is a low risk for suicide, and it is worth prioritising looking at hopelessness, as Beck has found that this predicts suicide but that CBT can prevent suicide (Brown *et al.*, 2005).

SUPERVISEE: I have been trying to focus on her hopelessness but it's hopeless! She can't see the point in doing anything.

SUPERVISOR: When you screened Margaret for depression did she indicate that she wanted treatment, didn't want treatment or didn't know?

SUPERVISEE: I didn't use the First Step Questionnaire. I just got on with the assessment and treatment of depression because it looked pretty severe.

SUPERVISOR: But the First Step Questionnaire (Scott, 2011) or the alternative 7-Minute Interview (Scott, 2011) would have alerted you to her ambivalence about treatment and this could then have been an immediate target.

SUPERVISEE: We are up to session seven and have got nowhere, though she does turn up.

SUPERVISOR: Let's role-play it: you take the part of Margaret and I'll be you and we will assume that Margaret ticked the 'don't know' box in response to the question about wish for treatment, and I will focus on the ambivalence, hopelessness and suicide risk.

SUPERVISEE: OK.

THERAPIST: What stops you going out and about as you did before the fall?

CLIENT: Why should I? Something's going to go wrong. I'm surprised I've reached 50 with all that has happened to me, others wouldn't. I wonder what is the point?

THERAPIST: Have there been any better times?

CLIENT: Yes, when I was working in Edinburgh 20 years ago.

THERAPIST: What about more recently?

CLIENT: I was a bit better for about six weeks before I tripped on the flagstone on my way to the bus stop.

THERAPIST: What was better in those six weeks?

CLIENT: I was putting my hair in rollers, cleaning the flat, taking my bike along the disused railway line, now I don't give a *****.

THERAPIST: Do you feel sad most of the day?

CLIENT: Yes, every day.

THERAPIST: How do you spend your day now?

CLIENT: I just sit there, at least I'm safe, I don't see why others see it as a problem. Can I come out of role now? It is at that point that I just want to shake her!

The role-play makes the thoughts and feelings of the supervisee more accessible than they might be from a purely intellectual discussion and it also gives the supervisor an opportunity to model the therapeutic process. Unless a supervisee has the opportunity to express their feelings the supervisory process is doomed to failure. The vignette continues:

THERAPIST: If you could choose a day like the day you had yesterday with the sort of day you were having in the six weeks before the fall which would you choose?

CLIENT: I know what you mean, but something is going to go wrong?

THERAPIST: You might be right, it is very difficult for any of us to foretell the future, but if it is going to go 'pear shaped' maybe that is even more reason for seizing the day and making the most of it.

CLIENT: Can I come out of role? You have picked up the ambivalence in a way in which I didn't and tackled it in a motivational interviewing (Bowden-Jones and Smith, 2012) way, implicitly challenging her sense of hopelessness and laid the ground for activity scheduling.

In the above exchange the supervisor has indicated how a more careful assessment could have identified more appropriate initial targets yet could also have ensured that the supervisee was adhering to a disorder specific protocol. Role-plays ought to be a regular feature of supervision helping ensure that the supervisor does not simply pontificate, providing a better learning experience for the supervisee. As such the supervisor is drawing on the explicit experiential learning model of Kolb (1984). A supervisor's credibility in large measure rests on the supervisee's perception as to how the former could perform with a client in the real world.

Chapter 8

Competence

It is taken as axiomatic that a supervisee must demonstrate competence, but attempts to measure 'competence' and relate it to outcome have proven problematic. The first section of this chapter is devoted to an examination of this issue and it is suggested that competence cannot be divorced from adherence. In the following sections different types of supervisee competence are distinguished: stage specific competences, diagnosis specific competences, and generic competences. It is suggested that these competences reciprocally interact, such that a deficit in one may nullify other competencies: see Figure 8.1.

Although the CBT 'car' is powered by a 'competence engine', this 'engine' is housed in a body of 'treatment adherence', and without both, travel is impossible. It is therefore suggested that the focus should be on assessing treatment fidelity, a composite of adherence and competence, and ways of operationalizing this are discussed.

The empirical justification for a focus on competence and adherence

The literature on adherence–outcome and competence–outcome suggests some caution is necessary in assuming there are significant correlations. Webb *et al.* (2010) in their meta-analyses of outcome studies found the correlations were not significantly different to zero. However, they also found considerable variability in the results from different studies and there did appear to be a significant correlation between competence and outcome when the focus was on depression (see Shaw *et al.*, 1999). More recently, Ginzburg *et al.* (2012) found, in a study of clients treated with CBT for social phobia, that competence of therapists as assessed by the Cognitive Therapy Competence Scale-Social Phobia predicted 48 per cent of the variance in outcome. Of the six individual competence items that significantly predicted outcome, four were specific to CBT for social anxiety disorder and two were more general CBT items ('interpersonal effectiveness' and 'pacing and efficient use of time'). More generally it would seem more appropriate to assess specific competences and generic competences separately. Ginzburg *et al.* (2012) note 'Competence presupposes a reasonably high level of

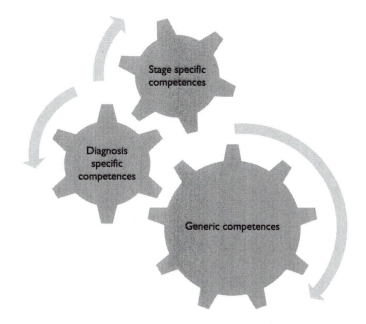

Figure 8.1 The competence engine.

adherence in the sense that one cannot be judged to have implemented a treatment well if the procedures specified in the manual were not used'. Despite this, in their study Ginzburg *et al.* (2012) found that adherence did not predict outcome. However, they observed their study was a randomised controlled trial, and as such there was little variability in adherence, whereas in routine practice variability is much more likely, and consequently a relationship between adherence and outcome would be in evidence.

Diagnosis specific competences

The diagnosis specific competences rest on an accurate assessment of the presence of disorder/s, and attempts to implement the evidence based protocol/s for the particular disorder/s. For depression and the anxiety disorders a set of disorder specific treatment targets and techniques are reproduced in Appendix D. The Treatment Adherence Scales can be adapted also to measure competence as well; as shown in Table 8.1, fidelity is a composite of adherence and competence.

A set of fidelity measures for depression and the anxiety disorders are reproduced in Appendix E. Following criteria elaborated by Rollinson *et al.* (2008), the three main criteria used to define 'competent' practice are that each therapeutic activity should be carried out in a manner that is clearly matched to the individual

Table 8.1 Treatment fidelity in depression

Treatment adherence and competence: Depression

Adherence: How thoroughly were specific treatment targets and techniques addressed in the session?:

1 Not done	2	3 Some discussion	4	5 Considerable discussion	6	7 Extensively discussed	Competence: How skilfully was the target addressed using the particular techniques? Rate 1–7, where 1 is no competence and 7 is total competence

Treatment target	Technique	Score
1. Depression about depression	Focus on responsibility for working on solutions and not on responsibility for problem	
2. Inactivity	Developing a broad investment portfolio, wide-ranging modest investments	
3. Negative views of self, personal world and future	Challenging the validity, utility and authority by which these views are held. Use of MOOD chart	
4. Information processing biases	Highlighting personal biases and stepping around them using MOOD chart	
5. Overvalued roles	Valuing multiple roles, renegotiation of roles in social context	
	Mean score	

client's presentation, individualized to their particular difficulties and carried out collaboratively. The CBT skills necessary to deliver effective CBT treatment for depression and the anxiety disorders are elaborated in Scott (2009). It should be noted that Rollinson *et al.* (2008) have produced a fidelity measure for the CBT treatment of psychosis, though for historical reasons it is inappropriately termed an adherence scale (Revised Cognitive Therapy for Psychosis Adherence Scale (R-CTPAS)).

In a review of CBT outcome studies Roth, Pilling and Turner (2010) found that almost universally therapists received model-specific supervision throughout treatment. In order to transfer the benefits of these efficacy studies to routine practice similar supervision is likely to be required. Roth and Pilling (2007) have detailed the competences necessary to deliver CBT for depression and the anxiety disorders, available online at www.uccl.ac.uk/CORE. These authors have detailed sets of disorder-specific competences, with in some cases alternative protocols when there is more than one evidence-based treatment for a disorder. The format of these competency guidelines is illustrated by the following extract from the OCD competence (Table 8.2).

The Roth and Pilling (2007) guidelines can, if necessary, be used to flesh out the briefer measures of disorder specific competences in the Treatment Fidelity Scales, in Appendix E or used by themselves.

Table 8.2 Extract fom OCD competence guidelines

Intervention

A capacity to engage the client with the intervention An ability to provide a general explanation of the aetiology and maintenance of symptoms, and to respond to the client's queries about this

An ability to describe and explain the rationale for the behaviour therapy program, and to respond to the client's queries about this

An ability to assess the client's motivation to engage in exposure and relapse prevention

An ability to ensure that homework planning and review occurs in all sessions

In vivo exposure An ability to work with the client to develop a hierarchy (or if relevant, multiple hierarchies) for exposure

An ability to revise the hierarchy in relation to the client's response (for example their actual, as contrasted to their predicted, response to each element), and as new information about obsessional discomfort becomes available during the intervention

An ability to implement direct exposures and adjust the duration of exposure to the needs of the client (as gauged by their self-reported anxiety levels)

An ability to help the client manage high anxiety during exposure

An ability to encourage clients fully to focus their attention on exposure situations

(Continued overleaf)

Table 8.2　(Continued)

An ability to use therapist modelling when this seems relevant

An ability to agree on homework tasks with the client at the end of each session

An ability to facilitate the client's taking responsibility for planning the exposures and carrying out homework, including identifying further situations that provoke obsessional discomfort, self-exposures and prevention of rituals

For clients who do not initially undertake self-conducted exposure in their usual surroundings, an ability to generalise symptom reduction from treatment site to natural situations

Imaginal exposure An ability to decide whether the addition of imaginal to in-vivo exposure is appropriate (usually offering this for clients whose fears predominantly involve mental images rather than external events, who report fears of disastrous consequences if they do not ritualise, or those whose fears are predominantly focused on harming others)

An ability to test the client's ability to bring to mind images which are vivid enough to permit exposure

An ability to construct a hierarchy and agree with the client specific content of each image

An ability to contract with the client to prevent neutralising rituals during the images, and if relevant to agree on strategies to ensure that these are not carried through

An ability to describe the exposure image as if it were happening in real time, and to encourage the client to use various sensory modalities (sight, sound, touch, smell) to retain a strong image and to become aware of emotional reactions to the events in the image

An ability to continue or repeat the exposure image in a vivid manner until the client's discomfort reduces noticeably (as gauged by the client's verbal report during the image)

Ritual prevention An ability to agree a plan for ritual prevention with the client, preferably by eliminating rituals, but modifying this as relevant to the client's presentation and capacity to tolerate this

An ability to help clients self-monitor and record rituals throughout the exposure process

An ability to work with the client to identify any previously unidentified "mental" rituals that emerge during exposure and to implement strategies to control or prevent these (e.g. implementing exposure through the use of loop tape)

An ability to discuss client anxieties about desisting from rituals, especially when these expose clients to taking a risk

Source: Roth and Pilling (2007).

Stage specific competences

There are competences that therapists need to display at key points in the client's trajectory through therapy; these include: those required for the initial evaluation, presentation of a credible rationale for treatment, engagement (including addressing motivational issues), re-evaluation at various points in therapy and relapse prevention towards the end of treatment.

The issues surrounding the reliability of an assessment have been discussed in the previous section. In summary there is no evidence that a reliable assessment can be made without asking questions about each symptom that comprises a diagnostic set. But clients first need the opportunity to tell the story of their difficulties in their own words, and this open-ended interview suggests possible diagnoses (a differential diagnosis). Assessment should be multi-axial with enquiry not only about psychological and personality disorders but also about the psychosocial stressors the client is under and also about their physical state. The initial evaluation usually takes place at the first interview but may take two sessions; the framework of Table. 8.3, adapted from Scott (2009), may be used to assess competence at this stage.

Table 8.3 Competence in initial evaluation

	Competence: How skilfully was this item addressed? Rate 1–7, where 1 is no competence and 7 is total competence
1. Open-ended interview, establishing rapport	
2. Use of screening devices e.g the 7 Minute Mental Health Screen, differential diagnosis	
3. Directly accessing each symptom in a diagnostic set, structured interview	
4. Discussion of diagnoses	
5. Appropriate psychometric tests	
6. Presentation of credible rationale for the disorder utilising self-help material	
6. Sharing of provisional case formulations of each identified disorder	
7. Inquiry regarding expectations of therapy	
8. Elicitation of negative attitudes regarding self, therapy or therapist	
9. Pinpointing most urgent and accessible problems, clarifying goals	
10. Define therapist role	
11. Define client role to practise mutually agreed strategies between sessions	
Mean score	

There is detailed exploration of the items in Table 8.3 in Chapter Three of *Simply Effective Cognitive Behaviour Therapy* (Scott, 2009). Clients need a credible story of their difficulties that also pinpoints ways forward. To facilitate generalisation from the therapy room to the client's world pertinent self-help materials should be given out, e.g. the free Survival Manuals available at http://www.routledgementalhealth.com/simply-effective-group-cognitive-behaviour-therapy-9780415573429. The framework of Table 8.3 can also be used when the prime focus of the session is stocktaking, a re-evaluation. At a minimum there should be routine re-evaluation mid-way through the planned sessions and at the end of treatment, but this should also be done if there is no progress after 5–6 sessions and at other enduring stuck points.

Post-treatment with the passage of time skills can be forgotten and the client needs a protocol to stop slips becoming full blown relapses. Thus the latter sessions conducted by the supervisee need to focus to a degree on relapse prevention. Across the disorders relapse prevention needs to be a focus; this involves the supervisee helping the client distil a personally constructed self-help 'manual', utilising key points from therapy and drawing on self-help books and computer-assisted materials. The content of relapse prevention session/s can be focussed around 'Recovered But. . . .' in Scott (2009), and is adapted in Table 8.4.

The diagnosis-specific competences and stage-specific competences are necessary constituents of a demonstration of competence but they are not sufficient; generic CBT skills also have to be in evidence. The next section focuses on generic competences.

Generic competences

Generic CBT competences can be rated using the single item in Table 8.5.

In their study of 14 highly trained therapists Huppert *et al.* (2001) used a similarly worded item to that in Table 8.5 to assess generic competence. They found that the mean competency of their therapists was 5.59 with a standard deviation of 1.06. thus these therapists' competency scores were clustered at the high end of the scale and this may be why this single item measure of competence was found not to predict outcome. It may be that in routine practice therapists' scores would be more uniformly distributed along the scale and it would then predict outcome. Another possibility is that the item needs some refinement and the author has added the wording in italics, relating to homework in Table 8.5, focussing attention on the setting and review of homework. Homework compliance has been shown to consistently predict outcome (Mausbach *et al.*, 2010; Kazantis *et al.*, 2000) and it may be that therapist competence in the setting and reviewing of homework is key to a demonstration of a generic competence. In a study of cognitive processing therapy (CPT) for PTSD, Galovski *et al.* (2012) found that the most frequently missed non-CPT-specific items were 'not problem solving about homework' (32 per cent missing) and 'homework review' (25 per cent).

Table 8.4 Competence in relapse prevention

	How skilfully were these items addressed? Use a scale 1–7, where 1 is no competence and 7 is total competence
1. Focus on and specification of possible triggers to relapse	
2. Focus on and specification of thinking involved in any slip	
3. Focus on and specification of behaviours likely involved in a slip	
4. Re-affirming the utilty of specific strategies already used successfully, in order to stop slips becoming full blown relapses	
5. Focus on the framework that the client is to use in the event of slips, normalising slips, developing an expectation that the gap between slips will get gradually longer	
6. Alerting the client to information processing biases that are common when people slip, e.g. 'I am either cured or suffering from full. . . .' and the distillation of more appropriate self-statements, e.g. 'I need to remind myself that it is only a question of regaining lost ground. I am not back at square one'.	
7. Provision of tangible self-help materials to be referred to in the event of a slip including the client's own Survival Manual, as well as highlighting sources of emotional support	
8. Focus on overall progress, and making decisions about possible further treatment	
9. Focussing on client's feelings about losing therapist contact	
Mean Score	

Homework ensures that clients practise and refine new skills outside the therapy session and that they can thereby change their real world functioning/symptoms. Monitoring the homework set by a supervisee is a way of determining whether the latter was able to distil the products of their discussion with a client in such a way that tasks were set that were specific enough as to potentially make a difference to the presenting problems. Given the advent of tablet computers it is possible for

Table 8.5 Assessment of generic competences

Competence is globally rated for each session with a single rating on a 7-point scale						
1	2	3	4	5	6	7
Clearly inadequate		Fair		Good		Excellent

A therapist is rated as excellent if he or she has warm, supportive, collaborative, Socratic style and was able to articulate the concepts clearly, making them personally relevant to the client *in the setting and review of homework*.

Source: Adapted from Huppert *et al.* (2001).

supervisees to easily print out a homework assignment for a client whilst retaining an electronic copy, making for ease of review at the next session. In addition copies of homework can be furnished to the supervisor for review, and this process fosters accountability, as the following vignette illustrates:

SUPERVISEE: I'd like to discuss Stan, he missed the last session, said he couldn't face doing anything. He's been staying at home, agonising about his future, what direction to go and scared to make any noise in his flat because of his noisy neighbour. Stan was 'dragged out' on one occasion by his friend to go bowling and he did enjoy this, so I emphasised that the one time he was a bit better was when he did something.

SUPERVISOR: Sounds good highlighting the link between action and mood.

SUPERVISEE: But getting a response from him was like getting blood out of a stone.

SUPERVISOR: Have you got the previous session's homework on your tablet?

SUPERVISEE: Yes, I'll just access it . . . there it is:

Homework November 23rd

Use MOOD chart for any dips in mood.

Work to a timetable, not how you feel.

See yourself as a fish swimming along, smile to yourself when you see the bait (your mum) and swim on by.

SUPERVISOR: Did you review this homework with him.

SUPERVISEE: No, I was put out by his saying he nearly didn't come to this session and I didn't want to alienate him further by chastising him for not doing his homework.

SUPERVISOR: Perhaps you would like to role-play Stan and see what it would have felt like for him if the session was played another way.

SUPERVISEE: OK.

THERAPIST: Looks like you played the last couple of weeks without a look at the skills in the Homework for November 23rd.

STAN: Yes, I didn't want to be thinking about it all the time.

THERAPIST: So if you used the MOOD chart you would have been thinking about the future even more?

STAN: Well, no because I was thinking about it all the time anyway.

THERAPIST: So the MOOD chart wouldn't make you think about the future more. Would it make you think about it less?

STAN: Don't think so.

THERAPIST: Let's have a look at it, sounds like your observed thinking was 'I can't stand all this uncertainty about how I should play my future'.

STAN: I like my art, would like to get a portfolio together for College, but the jobs in that area are few. I like cooking, might be better off doing a chef course.

THERAPIST: Who says that you should have a crystal ball and know what to do?

STAN: Only me.

THERAPIST: You could do a series of experiments and see what turns out best or you could peer into someone's crystal ball.

STAN: I suppose I should stop agonising and get on with doing.

THERAPIST: That is exactly what the final column of the MOOD chart is about, once you have come up with some second thoughts, e.g. trying to feel certain leads nowhere, you decide what to do and do it.

SUPERVISOR: How did that feel?

SUPERVISEE: I didn't actually feel chastised about not doing the homework, you just highlighted the relevance of it. I hadn't quite realised that using the framework of the MOOD chart there is an implicit stop to rumination after the second thoughts.

SUPERVISOR: In terms of the generic competence scale (Table 8.5) how do you think you fared?

SUPERVISEE: I didn't exactly stay with a review or setting of homework, but I was very sympathetic. I guess a 3/7 at most.

The above exchange illustrates that monitoring of a supervisee by accessing the homework that they have prescribed for a client not only meets the goal of accountability but serves as a platform for the development of a generic competence. This dialogue also highlights the importance of experiential learning for the supervisee, in this case via a role-play. In the role-play the supervisor is not only modelling a more appropriate intervention but is allowing the supervisee to test out his/her assumptions about the client. Supervisors have to be ever mindful of the dangers of being overly didactic.

Trepka *et al.* (2004) used a single measure of competence 'Using the scale 0–5 (0 inadequate, 1 mediocre, 2 satisfactory, 3 good, 4 very good and 5 excellent), please give an overall rating of this therapist's competence as demonstrated on this tape' to predict Beck Depression score at post-treatment and found a correlation of 0.47. This item was the global rating of competence from the Cognitive Therapy Rating Scale (CTRS) but curiously Trepka *et al.* (2004) did not report the correlation between the total CTRS score and outcome.

The most commonly used measures of CBT generic competences are the Cognitive Therapy Rating Scale (Young and Beck, 1980), freely available online from the Academy of Cognitive Therapy, and the Cognitive Therapy Rating Scale Revised (Blackburn *et al.*, 2001) and these have been used in routine practice to the exclusion of the assessment of stage specific competences and diagnosis specific competences. The strengths and limitations of the CTRS need a more careful analysis. The CTRS and associated manual are freely available online at the Academy of Cognitive Therapy.

Whilst therapist competence (as measured by the Cognitive Therapy Rating Scale) has been found to relate to outcome in cognitive therapy for depression (Shaw *et al.*, 1999), the effect is modest, accounting for just 19 per cent of the variance in outcome on a clinician administered measure and with no relation with self-report outcome measures. Further, the aspect of competence that was most associated with outcome was structure (this referred to setting an agenda, assigning relevant homework and pacing the session appropriately); by contrast general therapeutic skills or specific CBT skills did not predict outcome. The Shaw *et al.* (1999) study should at least caution against an overemphasis on skill at the expense of structure. It is not clear whether the results with a depressed population would generalise to other disorders, but in popular usage its applicability has been assumed. A study by McManus *et al.* (2012) looked at the levels of agreement between therapists and supervisors using the CTRS: whilst there were moderate correlations between the two, the ratings of the less competent therapists were significantly more in agreement with those of their supervisors than the ratings of the more competent therapists! These authors posit several possible explanations for these strange results. But the received wisdom is that supervisor's ratings of clinical performance are thought to have the greatest validity because they bear the closest relationship with client outcomes (Chevron and Rounsaville, 1983; Kuyken and Tsivrikos, 2009). If it is not the case that supervision is inadequate then this casts some doubt on the validity of the CTRS, but it may yet be that the quality of supervision is poor. Further the inter-rater reliability of the CTRS has been found to be poor, with one study showing intra-class correlation of less than 0.1, unless the assessors are trained together (Jacobson and Gortner, 2000). It is unlikely that in routine practice raters will have been trained together, so that in the use of the CTRS disagreements are likely. This raises the question of whether the penchant for using the CTRS has been a matter of the 'tail wagging the dog'. Perhaps the CTRS should not be regarded as a 'gold standard' in the present state of knowledge, rather it is a 'silver standard' and we are without a 'gold standard'.

It may be that measures of generic competence would fare better in predicting outcome, if they were not used to take a snapshot of a therapist's competence but first placed into context by the assessor/supervisor first viewing a DVD of the initial evaluation. Viewing a 'video' rather than a 'photograph' of a supervisee's competence may make for better recognition of their ability to make a significant difference with a client.

The supervision session is a laboratory in which differences between a supervisee's and a supervisor's assessment of competence can be critically examined, as the following vignette illustrates:

SUPERVISOR: I watched your DVD of the soldier who had returned from Afghanistan and you clearly have developed a great rapport.

SUPERVISEE: Jed is a very likeable guy, but he is having difficulty adjusting since leaving the army.

SUPERVISOR: On the relationship aspects of the CTRS I rated your performance high, but there was a conspicuous absence of guided discovery and I rated you low on this.

SUPERVISEE: I rated myself on Treatment Fidelity for PTSD (Appendix E, reproduced in Table 8.6 below).

SUPERVISOR: But that is measuring fidelity which is a composite of adherence and diagnosis specific competence.

SUPERVISEE: What is wrong with that?

SUPERVISOR: Nothing, I suppose we need to assess fidelity and generic competences.

SUPERVISEE: But there are also stage specific competences (Scott, 2012), and the CTRS Manual says the CTRS is not to be used for the initial evaluation, so there needs to be a different framework for assessing the first interview.

This vignette indicates that differences between supervisee and supervisor may be more to do with using different yardsticks at different points in time, than reflecting real differences in the assessment of competence. The dialogue continued:

SUPERVISOR: But there was no Socratic dialogue.

SUPERVISEE: I agree to a point, even if you used the single item measure of generic competence by Scott (2012) (Table 8.5), it does mention Socratic dialogue in passing but places more emphasis on the setting and review of homework and I gave myself a 5 on this scale.

SUPERVISOR: I can see how you would give yourself a 5 on that measure.

SUPERVISEE: The WET (Written Exposure Therapy, Sloan et al. (2012)) programme for PTSD is very prescriptive: after psychoeducation about PTSD, over the next five sessions there is 30 minutes each session devoted to the client writing about their trauma and its effects. To begin with, the writing is more about the trauma then gradually about the 'hotspots' and the effect of the trauma on their life. For homework they are asked to allow themselves to experience any trauma-related memories, images, thoughts or feelings between sessions; this fits in with the programme rationale of confronting the trauma memory rather than avoiding it.

Table 8.6 Treatment fidelity: PTSD

Treatment fidelity: Post-traumatic stress disorder

Treatment target	Technique	Adherence: How thoroughly were specific treatment targets and techniques addressed in the session?: 1 Not done, 2, 3 Some discussion, 4, 5 Considerable discussion, 6, 7 Extensively discussed		Competence: How skilfully was the target addressed using the particular techniques? Rate 1–7, where 1 is no competence and 7 is total competence
			Score	
1. Beliefs about PTSD	Normalisation of symptoms utilisation of Moving On After Trauma			
2. Cognitive and behavioural avoidance	Advantages and disadvantages short and long term of avoidance			
3. 'No one can understand what I've been through'	Realistic portrayal of discomfort 'to be expected. Underlining similarities of trauma and responses			
4. Managing reminders	The menu of options for handling reminders			
5. Behavioural avoidance. Fear of anxiety	Beginning the journey of a return to normality by gradual 'dares'			
6. Processing of traumatic memory	Written or verbal account of trauma and its effects elaboration of the memory			
7. Motivation	Motivational interviewing			
8. Rumination cognitive avoidance	Disturbed sleep/nightmares. Addressing the traumatic memory at a specific time and place			
9. Discrimination of triggers	Using similarities and differences			
10. Irritability, emotional avoidance and 'control freak'	Traffic light routine. Managing 'seething' over the trauma and its effects, coping strategies			

11. Persistent and exaggerated negative expectations of oneself, others or the world and persistent distorted blame of self about the cause or consequence of the traumatic event and core maladaptive schemas in PTSD	Use of MOOD chart to modify observed thinking and underlying assumptions. Use of magnifying glass analogy to illustrate exaggeratedly negative view of self, others and world
12. Cognitive avoidance Behavioural avoidance Hypervigilance for danger	Attention control and detached mindfulness. Continuing to 'dare'
13. Impaired relationships	Beginning to invest in people
14. Low mood, pain/disability View of self, world and future	Mood management strategies. Cognitive restructuring, the importance of a broad investment portfolio
	Mean score

SUPERVISOR: I need to look at the WET programme and consider whether it is evidence based.

SUPERVISEE: But on the Treatment Fidelity Measure, I've done exactly what is required: item 6, writing of a trauma has been part of a lot of CBT for PTSD.

SUPERVISOR: True, but it has always been a part of a package of cognitive restructuring. I suppose it is a bit like using the CTRS to assess a therapist doing CBT for a phobia: the standard behavioural approach which is evidence-based was not designed to be evaluated in terms of a therapist's ability to use guided discovery/Socratic dialogue.

This dialogue exposes the current dilemmas for supervisors in assessing a supervisee's competence: both have to be clear about which competence they are assessing and about the limitations of any measuring instrument for that competence. CBT is constantly evolving but not all new developments will withstand the test of time. There is an ever present danger of the adoption of a new approach because of the eminence or marketing skills of the originator; however, existing CBT treatments, particularly in routine practice, are often far from perfect and new approaches deserve careful scrutiny. The above vignette continues at the next supervision session:

SUPERVISOR: I had a look at the WET protocol (Sloan *et al.* (2012)) and it is certainly in the tradition of the writing assignments that have been part of Cognitive Processing Therapy for PTSD (see Resick *et al.* (2002)), it just specifies a particular way of doing the writing assignments . . .

SUPERVISEE: I sense a 'but' coming.

SUPERVISOR: Well, the subjects in the Sloan *et al.* (2012) study were media recruited and their traumas were motor vehicle accidents. Is that sort of protocol really going to work with a traumatised soldier from Afghanistan?

SUPERVISEE: We seem to be making some progress, but I felt I just couldn't leave him in the room by himself to write for 30 minutes as Sloan *et al.* (2012) did.

SUPERVISOR: I can see what you mean. I remember watching your DVD of the initial evaluation of this soldier. I remember vividly when he started describing the horrors of seeing his friend blown up he was in tears, stood up and said like a little boy 'I want to go now'. I think you did a brilliant job when you said something like 'we are not going to be going over the incident for the sake of it but instead be looking at better ways of handling the memory, because running from it doesn't seem to work'. He then sat down and you were able to continue the assessment.

SUPERVISEE: I suppose what I have done in using the WET protocol (Sloan *et al.*, 2012) is to go back on the rationale I used to engage him. Perhaps I should have used a non-trauma-focussed CBT intervention first and see if there is a need to step up to trauma-focussed.

SUPERVISOR: There is some limited evidence for the efficacy of a non-trauma-focussed coping skills CBT intervention (see Scott, 2012) but it is limited, and with Jed it might have helped to acclimatise him to the possibility of something like the WET programme (Sloan *et al.*, 2012).

The dialogue above indicates how having first viewed a supervisee's initial evaluation helps the supervisor make a more refined judgement about the competence exhibited in a treatment session. It also illustrates the need for the supervisor to model a measured approach to new developments.

Chapter 9

Group supervision

Group supervision provides the opportunity for the supervisee to learn not only from the supervisor but also from other therapists and can lessen the sense of isolation. It also appears a better use of the supervisor's time, but the author knows of no empirical evidence to support this. Group supervision is less flexible, in that the commitments of all members of the group have to be considered and usually sessions are scheduled to last an hour and a half, every four to six weeks. The difficulties in conducting group supervision in many ways mirror those of conducting group therapy. As in group therapy there is the ever-present danger of one member dominating the group, and of one or more members being disruptive to learning. Just as in conducting group CBT, the supervisor not only has to draw on a knowledge and experience of evidence-based protocols for different disorders/problems but must also be able to identify and manage group processes (Scott, 2011).

Supervision implies a differential in terms of power and knowledge; in peer supervision there is no such formal differential, yet it may, in group format, be a crucible for learning both didactically and experientially. Peer supervision does, however, differ from group supervision as the latter involves explicit monitoring and the supervisor is accountable to the funding body. Despite clear differences between peer supervision and group supervision, both will be affected by group processes and the management of these processes is likely to affect outcome.

This chapter begins with a consideration of the difficulties surrounding group supervision which can arise from non-selection of group members. It is suggested that the very diversity of group members can be a great challenge to the supervisor's management of group processes. In the following sections the pertinent aspects of managing group processes are delineated and the ways in which they can be orchestrated to enhance the learning of supervisees are elaborated.

Group composition

For most group supervisors, the formation of the group is opportunistic, e.g. CBT counsellors from the same charity. There is thus likely to be more heterogeneity in the group than would be found in group therapy where members are usually selected on the basis of their principal disorder/difficulty. Participants in group supervision may differ along numerous dimensions including experience, education, client group, with little in common except that they are expected to provide CBT. Given this diversity, creating group cohesion can be a major challenge and depends upon the effective management of group processes.

Group processes

Scott (2011) has codified a set of General Group Therapeutic Skills in the General Group Therapeutic Skills Rating Scale (GGTSRS). In Table 9.1 these skills are reframed for application in group supervision.

The management of the group processes in Table 9.1 is illustrated by reference to the characters in the fictitious supervision group in Table 9.2.

1. Review of 'homework'/agenda

Just as a review of homework ensures continuity between sessions in individual therapy, so to a review of 'homework' (agreed ways forward), Table 9.1 helps ensure refinement of supervisee's skills in group supervision. Without 'homework' the group supervision session can become an exercise in crisis management. Supervisees will usually almost certainly bring their current crises to the supervision session and it is right that these concerns should be placed on the

Table 9.1 Group supervisory skills

1. Review of 'homework'(agreed ways forward)/agenda
2. Relevance
3. Adaptation
4. Inclusion
5. Comprehensive elicitation of treatment targets
6. Magnifying support and minimising criticism
7. Utilising group members as role models
8. Supervisor presentation skills
9. Addressing group issues

Table 9.2 Group supervision members

Jamie	A clinical psychologist with ten years experience, working primarily in NHS adult mental health but with a small private practice
Caroline	A CBT therapist working in NHS adult mental health
Harry	A trainee counselling psychologist working across a number of charities
Louise	A CBT therapist working in child and adolescent mental health

agenda. Helping supervisees tackle 'hot' issues can greatly enhance the learning of new skills but a balance has to be struck between this and the steady development of a skill. The agenda set should reflect this balance.

2. Relevance

A pressing concern in group supervision is to ensure that the content of the session is relevant to each group member, most of the time. There is however necessarily some individualisation of a group session and this can promote group cohesion e.g. members of the group expressing their sympathy at the death of a member's parent. At times however there is a need to individualise the supervision but it may be difficult to do so within the confines of the group, as the following vignette involving the characters in Table 9.2 makes clear:

JAMIE: I've got a difficult case to discuss and I'm not even sure that I should be involved in it, it leaves a nasty taste. It is an ex-soldier who was in Iraq, he and two colleagues were told to go to a house where two known terrorists brothers were and arrest them. They went to the house and said the first names of the brothers; one of the occupants answered to the first name but said his brother was out. My client and his colleagues began interrogating him about membership of a particular group and for details of his brother; the man protested his innocence and said his brother was disabled; they began to manhandle him. They stripped him, threatened to shove a set of keys up his backside if he didn't give more information and the man defecated. They then searched the place and could find no evidence of any link to a terrorist organisation. After about an hour the brother arrived; he clearly suffered from cerebral palsy and after further enquiry they realised that they had the wrong address. Both brothers were distraught. My client feels so guilty about what he did and drinks to assuage it.

LOUISE: I wouldn't have any sympathy for him either, he deserves to feel *****.

JAMIE: But his PTSD is affecting his wife and kids.

HARRY: At least he is sorry for what he did. Who knows what any of us would have done if placed in that cauldron?

CAROLINE: It creates mixed emotions, anger that he has violated this guy, but his wife and kids are stuck with him and if only for their sake you have got to do something.

SUPERVISOR: I think that I would find it very difficult to take on such a case if he were simply complaining of flashbacks/nightmares of the incident without any contrition, but as Harry says I think his contrition makes a difference.

JAMIE: It raises the question: are we always here to take away every negative emotion, such as guilt?

SUPERVISOR: That's a really difficult one. I'd need to think about that and perhaps give you a ring about it, Jamie, but I would like to raise whether the chap's problem is actually PTSD, depressive rumination about the violation, or both, because depending on which it is you would go in different directions.

The above exchange illustrates the virtues of group supervision: a lessening of the supervisee's sense of isolation with their problem, and a greater breadth of credible opinion than would be the case in standard one-to-one supervision. There is, however, in group supervision the ever-present danger that the idiosyncratic concerns of one member might dominate the supervision session; in such circumstances 'relevance' and 'inclusion' (see Table 9.2) would have been poorly managed. In the vignette the supervisor has circumvented this by suggesting a one-to-one telephone conversation about a possibly idiosyncratic concern.

3. Adaptation

Supervisors need to be able to adapt the teaching of CBT to the diverse needs of supervisees, as the following dialogue illustrates:

LOUISE: I'm making progress with 10-year-old Omar. I'm 'daring' him to cross minor roads with Mum or Dad waiting on the other side, but he is afraid to go upstairs by himself of a night. I have tried dares about this and it doesn't work. His younger siblings will go upstairs by themselves.

JAMIE: What about going cognitive?

LOUISE: What do you mean?

JAMIE: Say getting him to use the MOOD Chart about his fears?

LOUISE: I don't think he would be up to it.

CAROLINE: You could do the experiment and see.

SUPERVISOR: I think there is necessarily a bit of experimentation in doing developmentally appropriate CBT. Conveying to young children the idea that it is your thoughts/images that largely create your fears can be very difficult; perhaps you might get all the children to construct (draw/paint) a collage of the horrible monster upstairs, get them to pin it up on an upstairs landing in the day and play dares going up and past it, then the same game of an evening and see how that works out.

In the above vignette supervisees draw on their own experience to help and motivate each other, whilst the supervisor synthesises their insights, adapting the material for use by the supervisee who raised their concerns. Without a tailoring of group supervision to the individual supervisee, supervision is likely to be impotent.

4. Inclusion

Inevitably some members of a supervision group are more vocal than others and some can feel, rightly or wrongly, intimidated by others. The supervisor's task is to ensure inclusion of all, and the following exchange illustrates some of the difficulties in achieving this:

SUPERVISOR: Did folks do a recording of a session?

CAROLINE: Sort of. I recorded it on a digital recorder, loaded it on my laptop and tried to send it as an e-mail attachment, but I got a message saying it was too big?

JAMIE: Just compress it.

HARRY: Or get a flash disc.

CAROLINE: A flash disc?

JAMIE: Just a drive you can buy almost anywhere.

LOUISE: Yes, it's one of these (*showing Caroline hers*), I got mine in W.H. Smiths for a couple of pounds.

In the above vignette, one of the group members appears to be being left behind, fortunately another group member has responded in such a way as to include this member and obviate the need for the supervisor to directly address the issue. This exchange illustrates that group members may implicitly address the group processes in Table 9.2 and that the burden of managing such processes does not fall entirely on the shoulders of the supervisor.

5. *Comprehensive elicitation of treatment targets*

In group supervision the very attempt to ensure each group member has a say can unwittingly pressurise the supervisor to take at face value a member's definition of the problem, address this and move on. But more detailed enquiry is needed to ensure that the supervisee's definition of the problem is comprehensive. In making wider enquiry the supervisor is modelling the conduct of a detailed assessment, illustrated by the following vignette:

CAROLINE: Martin says he has been depressed since he was about 15, but for no particular reason. He sees his family now and again and feels he doesn't fit in; he does shift work at a factory, feels he doesn't fit in there, because they like to talk about football and he doesn't. Martin split up with his partner some years ago, has a 9-year-old daughter whom he sees and is very fond of. He said that thoughts of his daughter stop him injuring himself. Until 18 months ago he went canoeing and on walks with the Ramblers.

JAMIE: Sounds like he is depressed, need to get him active working to his strengths.

CAROLINE: He keeps saying he needs to get himself sorted, but he just stays in his bedroom in a 3-bedroomed house; he lets out one of the other rooms to a friend.

HARRY: Does he see any other friends?

CAROLINE: No, not for the last 18 months.

LOUISE: I think you need to get him to work to a timetable, see friends, go canoeing, rambling.

CAROLINE: I've sort of tried the behavioural activation; it doesn't work.

SUPERVISOR: What is your case formulation?

CAROLINE: Well he is depressed; when I asked him questions about each of the DSM IV criteria for depression, he clearly met the criteria.

SUPERVISOR: So he is a 'case' of depression, is he a 'case' of anything else?

JAMIE: I don't think it is helpful labelling people.

SUPERVISOR: But when Caroline 'labelled'/diagnosed depression it gave her a way forward: behavioural activation/activity scheduling. Can you be certain that there is nothing else also going on that may suggest another/complementary way forward?

LOUISE: Maybe Caroline is under-confident marketing the behavioural activation?

SUPERVISOR: So is Caroline's problem skills, assessment or both? How could you test this out?

Historically in supervision the emphasis has been on the development of generic skills and within a group of CBT practitioners at least one member is likely to believe that they are the sole requirement for competent practice. In the exchange below the supervisor makes a case that they should be complemented by diagnostic and stage-specific competences but this does not meet with universal agreement, creating dilemmas for the framework to be used in assessing competence. The exchange continues:

HARRY: Maybe we could role-play with Caroline how she marketed the activity scheduling?

SUPERVISOR: Fine, we could do that. But what further questioning might be necessary to create a case formulation?

LOUISE: I'd like to know a bit more about his childhood.

SUPERVISOR: What evidence-based treatment would that suggest?

LOUISE: Well, if he had been abused.

CAROLINE: I asked him that and he said he hadn't.

JAMIE: I think with experience you get a feel for these cases, something's gone on in childhood.

SUPERVISOR: What is the evidence that an 'experienced hunch' is predictive?

JAMIE: Well it's better than being mechanistic.

HARRY: Maybe keep it simple by asking about alcohol/cannabis misuse in the last 18 months?

SUPERVISOR: I don't think that there is anything to beat a comprehensive screen as a first step to case formulation. Perhaps we should also role-play the assessment? We could use the framework of Table 8.3, Competence in an Initial Evaluation, to assess how we do.

JAMIE: Why not just concentrate on this client's strengths?

SUPERVISOR: What is the evidence base for doing just that?

JAMIE: There is a recent paper by Cheavens et al. (2012) that shows it is better to do that than concentrating on remedying deficits.

SUPERVISOR: That's true but that was in a sample where it had already been established by a standardised diagnostic interview that the principal disorder the clients were suffering from was depression; in the case of Caroline's client this is not yet known.

HARRY: I've got hold of the Competence in Initial Evaluation, (Table 8.3). I'd like to run through it perhaps with Caroline playing her client as she knows him best and you guys could give me feedback?

SUPERVISOR: Table 8.3 does not look mechanistic, but as you apply it Harry you could judge whether it feels that way.

LOUISE (*Looking at Jamie*): You cannot dismiss something without actually trying it.

The above vignette illustrates the need for a comprehensive assessment before embarking on treatment. Further that opposition to the inclusion of a standardised diagnostic interview is usually by those who have never or rarely used them. Rather than argue the whys and wherefores, the supervisor, in a spirit of collaborative empiricism, has suggested systematic experimentation with them.

6. Magnifying support and minimising criticism

It is – or should be – routine practice for therapists to first focus on what clients have done well, and praise this, before giving very specific feedback on how what has been done badly might be improved. Unless the client is first recognised and validated for what they have done well, they are likely to be too fragile to take on board any criticism, seeing the latter as a personal attack. Similarly the successes of a supervisee should be first praised before specific criticism is made, but in group supervision there is no guarantee that all group members will do this, as the following exchange illustrates:

HARRY: I've had a couple of sessions with a client, Madeleine, but I'm not sure where I'm going. She had a lot of discomfort after giving birth a year ago; three months later they operated and found a swab had been left in, and she is very anxious about becoming pregnant again, 'couldn't go through all that again', but then she would like a boy as she has two girls. I thought she had been traumatised so I assessed her for PTSD, using the DSM IV criteria, but there are no flashbacks or nightmares.

SUPERVISOR: It is always worth checking out for PTSD even if the trauma isn't quite like a serious RTA or armed robbery; you did well there. What else do you think might be going on?

HARRY: I didn't want to pathologise her reaction, just work on what she wanted. Using the mnemonic SMART, I thought a *s*pecific goal might be to help her make a decision about having another child, that would be *m*easurable, *a*ttainable, *r*elevant/realistic and *t*imely if we could agree over what period she would make the decision.

CAROLINE: We used to talk about SMART goals when I worked in the Civil Service.

JAMIE: What, and you never reached them?

CAROLINE: Maybe I wasn't SMART enough!

JAMIE: Oh dear!

SUPERVISOR: I think SMART can be a useful adjunct to problem solving, but by itself is it a stand-alone evidence-based treatment?

LOUISE: It is more like a technique. Were there any other disorders/difficulties that Madeleine has?

HARRY: She has the odd panic attack before and since the baby was born.

SUPERVISOR: Before the baby was born was she avoiding any situations because of the fear of panic attacks?

HARRY: Don't know.

SUPERVISOR: Does she avoid any situations now because of a fear of panic attacks?

HARRY: Don't know

JAMIE: Don't you think you should **** well find out?

SUPERVISOR: I don't think that there is any need for that, Jamie. It's very easy to get hooked by the one disorder you have in mind, make systematic diagnostic enquiry about that, but then only cursorily address others, when they don't fit in to your original pet theory.

In this vignette the supervisor strove assiduously to build up the confidence of group members, offer some degree of protection from excessive criticism, but at the same time mirror fidelity to what constitutes an evidence-based intervention.

7. Utilising group members as role models

With the best of intentions a supervisor may not be the best role model for a supervisee, and other members of the group may be closer in culture, education and experience to a group member. A group member's sense of self-efficacy can be more greatly enhanced by the coping model portrayed by another member than the perhaps masterful display of the supervisor. The following vignette illustrates this:

LOUISE: Serena is depressed, she and her partner split up a year ago because of his gambling and £4000 worth of debt he ran up, they had been together twelve years, they have a nine-year-old daughter and she has been obstructing access.

SUPERVISOR: Has the gambling been going on throughout their relationship?

LOUISE: No, only since he developed Parkinson's 18 months ago.

SUPERVISOR: Gambling and hypersexuality are sometimes side effects of levo-dopa (L-dopa) that is used to treat Parkinson's.

LOUISE: She didn't mention any sexual problems.

SUPERVISOR: Did you ask?

LOUISE: No, but she did say that since they reduced his medication, I don't know what it was, he stopped gambling, but she feels he is too needy, always on at her to get back together.

HARRY: Maybe she is too afraid of the responsibility of looking after someone with Parkinson's.

LOUISE: Serena said he shakes more since reducing his medication.

SUPERVISOR: Straightforward CBT for depression is an option but so too would be psychoeducation on L-dopa and cognitive behavioural marital therapy. In a study by Beach and O'Leary (1986) of depressed married women, one half were treated with individual cognitive behaviour therapy and one half with marital therapy (principally involving communication training) and the depression lifted equally in both groups.

LOUISE: Yes, I think I should perhaps get into some communication training with them even if it is at the level of a better modus operandi than getting back together at this stage.

HARRY: You are a braver person than I, I think my mind would go blank with so much going on in the same room.

SUPERVISOR: Maybe at our next supervision session Louise can tell me beforehand what has happened and she and I can role-play the couple and you can be the therapist and Caroline and Jamie can give you feedback?

HARRY: Only if Jamie is going to be civil.

JAMIE: I will do some homework on it!

The above dialogue illustrates that there can be a greater range of opportunities for experiential learning in group supervision but that they can come at a price. Further the vignette shows that it is not only necessary for the supervisor to have knowledge of group processes for group supervision but she/he also has to have an extensive knowledge base, i.e. that content is important as well as process.

8. Supervisor presentation skills

There is an ever-present danger in both individual and group supervision that the supervisor takes on the role of 'sage' dispensing wisdom, instead of facilitating learning. The teaching aspect of a supervisor's role is probably more in evidence in a group context, and like all good teachers the supervisor should use a variety of media to summarise and encapsulate teaching points. The following vignette illustrates this:

CAROLINE: Does anyone have problems getting clients to complete Thought Records? I wonder where they get the clients from who can separate thoughts from feelings and rate degrees of belief in their automatic thoughts and rational responses?

JAMIE: I once asked a leading luminary who was giving a presentation at the Annual Conference what proportion of her clients can complete a Thought Record; she looked at me blank, then said you just have to give examples.

SUPERVISOR: It would be interesting to each look back at our last ten cases and determine what proportion of Daily Thought Records (DTR) were completed properly.

LOUISE: I think it would be the exception rather than the rule.

JAMIE: So why doesn't anyone say this?

HARRY: Perhaps the Emperor has no clothes?

JAMIE: I think cognitive restructuring with them gets convoluted; it just makes people ruminate about their rational response.

SUPERVISOR: There is a simpler alternative to the DTR, which is to use the MOOD chart, Scott (2009) (see Table 9.3).

SUPERVISOR: The first column is about teaching the client to track their mood, rather like someone with heart problems might be asked to track their heart rate with an ambulatory monitor, the 2nd column 'observed thinking' are the client's first thoughts associated with a dip in mood, the 3rd column 'objective thinking' is the client's likely better second thoughts. The final column asks the client to change gear, stop ruminating once they have come up with their second thoughts, decide what to do, and do it.

JAMIE: I like that it fits more in with a behavioural activation framework

In this exchange the supervisor has distilled tangible expressions of the fruits of the group supervision discussion, in suggesting a review of the acceptability of DTRs and usage of the MOOD chart. A supervisor with good presentation skills answers the specifics as to how a supervisee can make a difference and makes frequent use of metaphor, e.g. 'change gear', 'second thoughts'.

9. Addressing group issues

There can be relatively simple group issues like sorting out a convenient time to meet and more complex ones, involving conflict, that may affect the cohesion of the group. At its worst, one member may feel 'either he/she goes or I go', but usually there are early warning signs of such conflicts which can be prevented from escalating by taking the alleged offender to one side and problem solving

Table 9.3 MOOD chart

Monitor mood	Observe thinking	Objective thinking	Decide what to do and do it

different ways of responding. The supervisor has to budget that given the usually indefinite time scale of the supervision group, conflicts are inevitable and if ignored threaten the viability of the group. A useful starting point for conflict resolution is to suggest that the group has a common goal, to make each member a better therapist, and any one member's actions should be assessed on whether they advance or retard the realisation of this goal.

Chapter 10

Supervising dissemination and complexity

Historically clients seen by mental health service personnel have been the tip of the iceberg. In the UK this led to the development of Improving Access to Psychological Therapies (see, for example, IAPT, 2008) and a call for the greater dissemination of CBT (Shafran *et al.*, 2009). Hitherto supervisors have not been tasked with encouraging dissemination, but without their input, dissemination is less likely. This new facet to a supervisor's work requires skills with regard to less intense interventions, such as group work and guided self-help, but there has been little training of supervisors in these modalities. Group CBT has continued to be the exception rather than the rule, despite cost savings of the order of 40–50 per cent compared to individual therapy and evidence for equal effectiveness across most depression and anxiety disorders (Scott, 2011) and for bulimia and the addictions. Supervisors can play a pivotal role in nudging group CBT onto the therapeutic agenda. Instead, in recent years the focus of supervisors and CBT courses has been much more on helping supervisees manage 'complex' cases. The first section of this chapter focusses on helping a supervisee capitalise on the strengths of group work but how also to avoid the pitfalls. In the following section it is suggested that the proper management of group supervision can heighten a supervisor's awareness of aspects of group processes that are equally pertinent for group CBT and act as a stepping stone for delivery of the latter. In the final section of this chapter it is suggested that the term 'complex' is often ill-defined and can serve as a distraction to the provision of EBTs, but that complex cases can usually be dealt with by interweaving EBTs.

Groups and dissemination

Groups are an attractive option for Service Managers, making for a greater throughput of clients. For depression and the anxiety disorders group CBT and individual CBT appear equally effective (Scott, 2011), but the interventions examined have largely been diagnosis specific. Thus whilst there may be managerial pressure to admit all-comers, this is not an evidence-based approach, and the following vignette illustrates the difficulties supervisees may experience:

SUPERVISEE: My boss wants me to run an anxiety/depression group, the first four sessions on anxiety and the last four on depression.

SUPERVISOR: How do you feel about this?

SUPERVISEE: The thought of having someone in the group with OCD or PTSD and others who are largely worriers, seems daft. They are such different problems that in attending to one I would be neglecting the other, it will be stressful and you are going to get lots of dropouts.

SUPERVISOR: With such a mixed group it could be difficult to tailor the group sufficiently to the individual member.

The above example illustrates how the push to wider dissemination of CBT by using groups may have unintended negative consequences. Yet the cost savings for a diagnosis specific group are as much as 50 per cent (Scott and Stradling, 1990) and properly implemented group therapy widens the benefits of CBT. It is not, however, a panacea, and there can be problems with assignment to, and retention in, group CBT. Scott and Stradling (1990) addressed these difficulties by offering up to three individual sessions to run alongside the group programmes. In later work Scott (2011) has suggested that though groups should be diagnosis specific, the presence of additional disorders can be addressed by using e-mail/telephone calls, using freely available self-help materials for the comorbid disorders available from the Routledge website (http://www.routledgementalhealth. com/simply-effective-group-cognitive-behaviour-therapy-9780415573429). At the following supervision session, the discussion about implementing a group programme continued:

SUPERVISEE: I have been looking at employing a transdiagnostic approach to the running of groups (Norton and Barrera (2012)). Initially I was quite enthusiastic, but then discovered that the 'transdiagnostic' was confined to clients with panic disorder, social anxiety disorder and generalised anxiety disorder.

SUPERVISOR: I can see that with clients with panic disorder and social phobia you might have sufficient overlap in their difficulties that running a group for them might be feasible.

SUPERVISEE: Yes, it might be, but I also found that 74 per cent of those in the study had completed some or all of a degree/professional course; that is not at all the sort of population that I am dealing with.

SUPERVISOR: But the Scott and Stradling (1990) study of depressed clients, involving a comparison of individual and group CBT, with a waiting list was conducted in an inner city health centre, so there is some evidence for the external validity of group treatments. But I take your point: care would have to be taken in extrapolating the results from one setting to another.

SUPERVISEE: Norton and Barrera (2012) seem to be saying that their 'transdiagnostic' intervention is as good as the disorder-specific programmes for panic disorder, social phobia and generalised anxiety disorder.

SUPERVISOR: I've also had a look at their paper, and they had 23 clients assigned to diagnosis-specific group CBT but 48 per cent (11) of these were lost to follow-up; this is an unusually high level of losses in group CBT. In the transdiagnostic group they lost 30 per cent (7) to follow-up. Usually when there are dropouts the practice is to conduct an intention to treat analysis, which basically involves giving dropouts the same score at the end of treatment as their last recorded score. But as far as I can see Norton and Barrera (2012) didn't do this. I would be surprised, given the level of dropouts, that it was possible to detect a moderate difference between the diagnostic specific and transdiagnostic interventions.

SUPERVISEE: So you are saying that their not finding a difference between the transdiagnostic and diagnostic-specific intervention is more to do with statistics.

SUPERVISOR: I'm not a statistician, but it is a possibility. You would also have to look at allegiance effects: the originators of the study are committed to a transdiagnostic intervention and did the supervision, not only of the transdiagnostic arm but also of the diagnostic-specific arm, and there is a suggestion of more and unusually large fallout from the latter. In terms of the Chambless and Hollon (1998) criteria (*Appendix C*), this 'transdiagnostic' treatment would be regarded as only 'possibly efficacious'.

SUPERVISEE: In their generalised anxiety disorder groups, they had two groups of three clients, that's not the usual number for a group.

SUPERVISOR: It raises a problem for the typicality of their diagnostic-specific interventions, but in fairness with such low numbers perhaps one would have expected this to buttress the power of the diagnosis-specific interventions.

SUPERVISEE: A limited 'transdiagnostic' seems a definite 'maybe'.

SUPERVISOR: I also noticed that Norton and Barrera (2012) hit a common problem; when you wish to assign people to just a group intervention, of those that met criteria for their groups a third either refused to participate in the groups or did not materialise. This means special attention has to be paid to the marketing of groups and motivational strategies. Scott (2011) has described this.

SUPERVISEE: It would ease matters if I could put, say, panic disorder and social phobic clients in the same group.

SUPERVISOR: It would ease the logistics, but if you have a big enough catchment area it shouldn't be a problem getting sufficient clients of any one disorder.

In this vignette the supervisor has taken pains to ensure that in the understandable rush to give away CBT to as many as possible the quality of the intervention does not suffer. The supervisor has not shied away from the 'engineering' aspects of delivering group CBT in routine practice; inattention to these details can result in sub-optimal treatment.

Modelling group CBT in group supervision

For many supervisors and supervisees, group CBT is new terrain: unfortunately stand-alone workshops or workshops at conferences are rare and it is rarely addressed on courses. However, group supervision provides a useful laboratory in which group skills can be refined, as the following vignette illustrates, using the same cast of supervision group members from Chapter 9:

JAMIE: Right, so I'm the group leader and it is the second session of a depression group.

SUPERVISOR: Yes, if everybody could just be the last depressed client you met, and we can see how it goes for 15–20 minutes and then have a discussion on it.

JAMIE: Just to recap, at the end of the last session we looked at Activity Scheduling, timetabling in what might give you a sense of achievement and pleasure and I would like to go over how that worked out first and then go on further in the Depression Survival Manual, http://www.routledgementalhealth.com/simply-effective-group-cognitive-behaviour-therapy-9780415573429, to look at how your thinking affects your feelings. Is there anything else that folks would like to put on the agenda?

SUPERVISOR: I nearly didn't come.

JAMIE: Why was that?

SUPERVISOR: Didn't really have the money for the train, with the way the Government has cut back on benefits.

CAROLINE: It is ****, who is going to employ me, I've not worked for years.

LOUISE: Working is not everything; I was basically demoted when I had to apply for my own job even though I'm on the same pay.

JAMIE: The great thing is (*looking at the supervisor*) you came to the session, you did something, despite it being difficult. That is what the Activity Scheduling we did last time was about.

SUPERVISOR: I haven't done anything else.

JAMIE: Why?

SUPERVISOR: Money.

JAMIE: I thought you were going to go for long walks last time?

SUPERVISOR: Didn't bother, weather has been ****.

LOUISE: Haven't you heard of coats!

JAMIE: Can we stop there? I'm running out of steam.

SUPERVISOR: That tends to happen in groups, your mind goes blank, and having a co-leader is useful. What did it feel like, Jamie?

JAMIE: Like going up an increasingly steep hill, struggling to keep the bike on the road.

SUPERVISOR: I think you did well, in having a common reference for the group, a Survival Manual, and you persisted with a review of the homework, Activity Scheduling, even when I was being unhelpful.

CAROLINE: I thought Jamie kept to appropriate content despite bad weather on the hill.

JAMIE: Thanks Caroline.

HARRY: But somehow I couldn't get a look in, you two (*looking at Jamie and the supervisor*) got locked in gladiatorial combat.

JAMIE: I hadn't realised that, but looking back I can see what you mean.

SUPERVISOR: That highlights a major problem in group CBT: a need to attend not only to the appropriate content, targets and treatment strategies for the particular disorder but also to attend to group processes, one of which is Inclusion (see Table 10.1), Harry felt excluded.

A list of general group therapeutic skills, from Scott (2011), is reproduced in Table 10.1.

It is, of course, possible to simply ask a supervisee to read about managing group processes, but the material comes alive if preceded by a simulated group session. Further simulations can then take place in which the supervisee's skills are refined with the feedback of the supervisor and other supervisees. The group supervision session continued:

SUPERVISOR: Perhaps at the next supervision session we could role-play a session, (using Table 10.1), but also being mindful of the stage-specific competence for relapse prevention (Table 8.4).

JAMIE: The competences for relapse prevention (Table 8.4) do make it clear what I would need to be doing in the session, but looking at today's performance I think I will struggle.

SUPERVISOR: If we judged Jamie's performance today using the generic competence scale (Table 8.5, reproduced in Table 10.2 for ease of reference), what would folks make of Jamie's performance?

Table 10.1 General group therapeutic skills

1. Review of homework/agenda
2. Relevance
3. Adaptation
4. Inclusion
5. Additional disorders
6. Magnifying support and minimising criticism
7. Utilising group members as role models
8. Therapist presentation skills
9. Addressing group issues

Table 10.2 Assessment of generic competences (reproduction of Table 8.5)

Competence is globally rated for each session with a single rating on a 7-point scale

1	2	3	4	5	6	7
Clearly inadequate		Fair		Good		Excellent

A therapist is rated as excellent if he or she has warm, supportive, collaborative, Socratic style and was able to articulate the concepts clearly, making them personally relevant to the client *in the setting and review of homework.*

Source: Adapted from Huppert *et al.* (2001).

LOUISE: I thought it was good he followed through about you (*looking at supervisor*) not doing your homework but was quite Socratic about it.

HARRY: Yes I liked Jamie's bemused style 'I thought you . . .', mind you, Louise was just the opposite telling you (*looking at supervisor*) off like a naughty child, which threw Jamie.

CAROLINE: I think that it was probably a 5/7 on the generic competence scale until you ground to a halt.

SUPERVISOR: I agree.

JAMIE: That's encouraging.

The above dialogue illustrates the use of simple assessment devices to help supervisees structure and evaluate the learning of group CBT skills.

The complexity of 'complex'

There is no agreed definition of complex CBT, but it is a term applied variously, to the treatment of clients with a Severe Mental Illness (SMI – psychosis, bipolar disorder and depressive psychosis) and/or personality disorder or a client with significant comorbidity or a difficult to treat client. This raises the question of whether 'complex' refers to a property of the client, and if so, which properties? or does it refer to whatever case the therapist finds challenging. The term 'complex' is used to justify departure from standard CBT but this means moving away from Evidence Supported Treatments (ESTs). A lack of clarity about the meaning of 'complex' may result in inappropriate treatment. The following vignette illustrates the handling of these difficulties when they surface in supervision:

SUPERVISEE: Dealing with Bernard is quite a challenge: he was on patrol on foot when a car was driven at him, his colleague was 25 yards away in an armoured vehicle and did nothing. Bernard scrambled to avoid being hit by the car but sustained injuries and the ongoing pain has meant he has had to be invalided out of the Forces. He keeps going on about his colleague smiling at him as he lay on the floor after the incident. It is a complex case and recently I have been looking at his pain management

SUPERVISOR: Complex?

SUPERVISEE: Yes, there's lots going on: PTSD in relation to the car being driven at him, anger at his colleague and the Forces not providing any help, drinking too much and pain.

SUPERVISOR: So what were you doing with Bernard at the last session?

SUPERVISEE: I've recorded it, perhaps we could listen to some of it and you could give me feedback?

SUPERVISOR: Fine (*both listen to 30 minutes of the recording and then the supervisor continued*), you clearly had a great deal of rapport with Bernard and he feels he had benefitted from previous sessions, had particularly enjoyed the relaxation exercise. You seem to have based the session around the Coping Strategies Questionnaire [CSQ, Rosentiel and Keefe (1983)] and Bernard has indicated on a scale 0–6 [0 never do, 3 sometimes and 6 always do that when in pain] how much he engages in various strategies when in pain and any strategy he always or almost always uses you have asked him to explain why. But I wasn't clear where you were going with this.

SUPERVISEE: Well, when I asked him to explain his endorsement of 'it's terrible and I feel it's never going to get any better' he said that he imagined himself being in a wheelchair and I then asked him what his Consultant had said and it turned out this is not what the Consultant had said.

SUPERVISOR: But you left it at he should just listen to his Consultant, rather than putting it Socratically 'how do you square what you say to yourself with what your Consultant is saying?'

SUPERVISEE: That's true, I suppose in terms of the generic competence (Table 10.2) I didn't do well, but there was some homework setting, I asked Bernard to rate his pain levels and what he was doing.

SUPERVISOR: You did, but you set no homework on Bernard managing his mood despite his saying that his mood affected his pain.

SUPERVISEE: Maybe a 4/7 for generic competence.

SUPERVISOR: I think so, but there were no diagnosis specific competences in evidence. If he is suffering from PTSD, there was no focus on a treatment target specific to that condition, e.g. flashbacks/nightmares, and no focus on a matching treatment strategy, e.g. writing about the incident and its effects.

SUPERVISEE: I had done that at previous sessions.

SUPERVISOR: Why didn't you review the writing/flashbacks/nightmares at this session?

SUPERVISEE: I gave him the CSQ at the previous session to bring in and I thought we would look at that because of his pain.

SUPERVISOR: But you didn't determine beforehand the likely treatment targets and treatment strategies for pain, you were not following any EST for pain.

SUPERVISEE: Well, I was individualising it with the CSQ.

SUPERVISION: But you didn't seem to have looked at the studies/protocols of CBT for chronic pain.

SUPERVISEE: I was going by my formulation.

SUPERVISOR: A review of the literature on CBT for chronic pain concluded 'CBT may have a weak effect in improving pain, mood and disability in adults with chronic pain' [Eccleston *et al* (2009]. The 'complexity' seems to have arisen largely from not using ESTs and not looking at the literature.

The above vignette suggests that complexity is sometimes not so much a feature of the client but of the view the supervisee takes of the client if reference is not made to ESTs and the literature for the established conditions. Scott (2012) has provided a detailed example of how a client with multiple comorbidities, including a borderline personality disorder, can be treated simultaneously using ESTs.

It is doubtful whether the clients subsumed under the category of 'complex' have sufficient in common that they should be recipients of any one intervention. It is generally agreed that cases of Severe Mental Illness (SMI – psychosis, bipolar disorder and depressive psychosis) are more difficult to treat successfully with CBT than cases of depression, panic disorder, obsessive compulsive disorder, etc. but this does not make the former 'complex' per se; it is simply that the CBT treatment for those conditions is less of a panacea. In using the term 'complex', there is an implication that if the therapist was skilful enough he/she could treat the client with an SMI/chronic pain successfully and the supervisee may personalise their lack of success.

Chapter 11

Supervision of supervisors

The CBT therapist who wishes to develop his/her supervisory skills has available a menu of workshops/courses with varying degrees of allegiance to a CBT framework. Even explicitly CBT supervision workshops/courses may vary in their emphasis on formulation vs. diagnosis-specific protocols. Attendees at a supervision course/workshop may therefore have different definitions as to what they are about; some of these definitions may be congruent with those of the organisers, others may not. It can be asserted that there are certain core processes involved in supervision, in which the potency of supervision lies, and these are therefore justifiably the focus in supervision training. But the evidence base for the efficacy of supervision as a whole, much less its components, is slender, making a focus on the 'active ingredients' of the process problematic. Yet, in the interest of Continuing Professional Development the CBT therapist is likely to ultimately find themselves on a supervisory workshop/course. In this chapter the focus is on normalising a would-be supervisor's response to the vagaries of supervision training and on suggesting what should be the essential ingredients of supervision training. The difficulties for would-be and actual supervisors attending such courses/workshops are highlighted in the following fictional group (Table 11.1).

Table 11.1 Cast of supervision workshop

Martina – workshop leader	Clinical Psychologist, twenty years experience, eclectic/ transdiagnostic therapist.
Dave	Accredited CBT therapist, believes the supervisory, like the client relationship, is all important.
Jill	Accredited CBT therapist, believes in evidence based treatment, keen on groupwork and self-help.
Len	A clinical psychologist working towards BABCP accreditation.
Stephanie	A trainee counselling psychologist working towards chartered status.

At a supervision workshop the following exchange takes place:

MARTINA: I would like to look at the following dimensions of the supervisory relationship:

SUPERVISOR: The dimensions of the supervisory Relationship Questionnaire (SRQ) are a useful guide in assessing the function of a supervisor. Milne *et al.* (2011) have suggested that experiential learning is more powerful than didactic learning and he makes a distinction between evidence-based clinical supervision [EBCS] and CBT supervision. Following on from Milne (2011), I would like to role-play my being a supervisee bringing a case to supervision, one of you could be the supervisor and we could then discuss how the supervisor has done with regard to Table 11.2.

DAVE: Table 11.2 seems to sum up what I would think important for supervisors to attend to.

STEPHANIE: It would have been useful to ask our supervisees to complete the SRQ before coming along to the workshop; there could be a gap between how we think we are doing and how they think we are doing.

LEN: But the supervisees might just be wanting to be polite?

JILL: That's a difficulty but perhaps we could ask them to complete them before the follow-up workshop.

MARTINA: That could make for a very interesting discussion at the next workshop, but can we focus now experientially? Milne (2008) has pointed out that only 6–20 per cent of supervision sessions are experiential, involving listening to recordings/role-plays, and suggests this proportion should be greater in view of Kolb's (1984) learning cycle, with its cycle from concrete experience, through observation and reflection, to abstract conceptualization, and on to testing of those ideas in new situations. Hmm, I'm drifting into being didactic, let's go with the role-play, who would like to volunteer to be my supervisor?

Table 11.2 Dimensions of the supervisory relationship

	Examples
Safe base	'My supervisor was respectful of my views and ideas'
Structure	'Supervision sessions were structured'
Commitment	'My supervisor paid attention to my spoken feelings and anxieties'
Reflective education	'My supervisor drew from a number of theoretical models flexibly' and 'My supervisor encouraged me to reflect on my practice'
Role model	'I respected my supervisor's skills'
Formative feedback	'My supervisor's feedback on my performance was constructive'

Source: Palomo, Beinart and Cooper (2010).

The above vignette illustrates the emphasis on experiential learning, the supervisory relationship and the supervisory process in supervision training and is underscored by the following dialogue:

DAVE: I don't mind being the supervisor

MARTINA: OK, a bit of background. I work with a lot of abuse victims and I see the full range of adult mental health problems. Gina has been referred to me by her GP suffering from depression, her third marriage has broken up and she disclosed for the first time that she was raped at age 12; she is a successful businesswoman in IT. Let's start.

MARTINA: I would like to talk through my work with Gina, she is a formidable woman, takes no prisoners.

DAVE: How do you feel when you are with her?

MARTINA: Anxious.

DAVE: What makes you anxious?

MARTINA: That if I don't say just the right thing she will eat me alive, I think she probably ate her three husbands.

DAVE: Are you serious?

MARTINA: Well figuratively, not actually cannibalism.

DAVE: How does she explain the break-up of the marriages?

MARTINA: The first one she said they were just both too young, she was ambitious, he wanted a quiet life in suburbia. The second marriage lasted 5 years and there were periods when it was good but it fell apart when he was unfaithful. The third marriage lasted weeks, friends had advised her not to marry so quickly after meeting the guy and she soon realised that he was only after her money.

DAVE: That doesn't quite sound like a 'cannibal'?

MARTINA: I suppose it is just me, she is highly educated, 'posh'.

DAVE: And you are?

MARTINA: I get by, did the CBT course OK, but think someone might just discover I'm an imposter.

DAVE: So you fear Gina might unmask you?

MARTINA: Sounds silly, doesn't it?

DAVE: Doesn't stop it feeling frightening.

MARTINA: Maybe I should just carry this fear of being unveiled rather than see it as a threat.

DAVE: That might be the adaptive metacognitive approach.

MARTINA: If we could just stop it there and do a review of the dialogue so far using the SRQ.

STEPHANIE: You certainly tuned into the supervisee's anxieties, in terms of the SRQ there was commitment.

JILL: I think you also made her feel safe, a 'Safe Base' on the SRQ when she was inviting you to be dismissive.

LEN: There was also 'reflective education' on the SRQ, you did a Columbo-style bemused befuddlement, juxtaposing the supervisee's view of the client's marriages with what the client actually said, so within a CBT framework it was quite Socratic.

DAVE: Yes, though I was staying within a CBT framework, I can see that the SRQ was nevertheless useful.

MARTINA: I think you did well, I felt listened to and safe. I don't think the supervisory process and CBT are incompatible. There is an interesting paper by Gordon (2012) which is about supervisory processes from a CBT perspective and perhaps we can look briefly at that before continuing the role play (see Table 11.3).

MARTINA: We could look at the exchange we have just had within the framework suggested by Gordon (2012): he suggests that you can take a five-minute section of a supervisee's recording dealing with a particular issue and give important feedback on that. Reflecting on the role-play, how well was step 1 done?

DAVE: I suppose I never explicitly stated what the supervision question was.

Table 11.3 Ten steps for supervision

Step
1 Clarify the supervision question. *Aim for a clear question which will promote learning.*
2 Elicit relevant background information. *Keep it brief and structured, e.g. client problem statement, key points of history, formulation and progress to date.*
3 Request an example of the problem. *This will usually include listening to a session tape extract.*
4 Check supervisee's current understanding. *This establishes their current competence and gives an indication of the 'learning zone' where supervision should operate.*
5 Decide the level or focus of the supervision work. *For example, a focus on micro-skills, or problem conceptualization, or on problematic thoughts and feelings within therapist.*
6 Use of active supervision methods. *Role-play, modelling, behavioural experiment, Socratic dialogue.*
7 Check if the supervision question has been answered. *Encourage the supervisee to reflect and consolidate the learning.*
8 Format a client-related action plan. *Formalize how the learning will be used within the therapy.*
9 Homework setting. *Discuss any associated development needs, e.g. reading related literature or self-practice of a CBT method.*
10 Elicit feedback on the supervision. *Check for any problems in the supervision alliance, or learning points for the supervisor.*

Source: Gordon (2012).

STEPHANIE: But nevertheless you did help the supervisee to clarify whether the problem was an actual threat or felt threat.

DAVE: Yes, I couldn't focus it quite as sharply as that.

MARTINA: I think you did good enough, Dave, it is always easier looking back.

DAVE: Thanks.

MARTINA: On Step 2 I provided the background information, for Step 3 we had a live session rather than recording. Not sure we addressed Step 4 in this role-play.

JILL: Perhaps Dave did, because he came up with a game plan addressing the fear of being discovered to be an imposter: just accept the feeling and attach no personal significance to it; isn't that a 'learning zone'?

MARTINA: I guess so; what about Step 5?

LEN: Dave focussed on the supervisee's problematic feelings/thoughts, so Step 5 is OK and we were doing role-play anyway, so Step 6 is fulfilled.

STEPHANIE: We didn't answer the 'truth' or not of the supervisee being an 'imposter', so I'm not sure we did Step 7.

LEN: But we did look at how to handle the feeling of being an imposter.

JILL: Maybe this goes back to not being too clear as to what the supervision question was in the first place.

MARTINA: Maybe we don't have consensus around Step 7, but I don't think that matters too much: the steps are just guidance based largely on experience with not a lot of data to support them; we shouldn't turn them into tablets of stone.

DAVE: I think I managed Step 8, a client-related action plan, and I think it was pretty implicit that this was a homework Step 9.

LEN: Yes, you were really suggesting that the supervisee have a detached mindfulness about the feelings of being an imposter.

JILL: But you didn't actually say that to her, Dave. Why?

DAVE: For some reason I assumed it was a fairly new CBT therapist, who may well not have encountered a metacognitive approach in any depth.

MARTINA: So what you were doing, Dave, was implicitly altering the level of supervision to match the supervisee's knowledge base, rather as we do with clients anyway.

DAVE: I guess so, but I wasn't really conscious of doing so.

MARTINA: I think we are doing Step 10 as we speak. The learning point might be that you can sometimes do good things intuitively without really realising. I think it was Pascal who said 'the heart has its reasons that the mind does not know about'.

LEN: Yes, it is quite a useful framework.

In the exchange above, the workshop leader is modelling the integration of didactic teaching with experiential work, but as the role-play unfolds some tensions between a CBT framework and a traditional supervisory framework arise:

MARTINA: I find Gina exhausting, I asked her about the rape when she was aged 12 and she said she hadn't ever told anyone. When I asked her how it had affected her she said she became quieter and more introverted than she was and she was bullied a lot at school.

DAVE: You see a lot of trauma victims?

MARTINA: I suppose I do.

DAVE: How do you find that?

MARTINA: It gets a bit boring dealing with those who have had serious RTAs and often just have travel anxiety.

DAVE: What about looking after you?

MARTINA: I think that I am pretty good at switching off outside work, but I did think about Gina.

DAVE: Vicarious traumatisation is often an issue for trauma workers and they need to work on grounding themselves, watching how many cases they take on.

MARTINA: Could we pause there? What did folks make of that, using the frameworks we discussed?

LEN: Well, I would give Dave full marks for the supervisory relationship as on the SRQ but I'm not sure that within the Ten Steps (Table 11.1) he was addressing the question the supervisee was raising.

JILL: I am uneasy about the evidence base for vicarious traumatisation. I accept that you can have, say, a policewoman suffering from PTSD because she has spent ages looking at horrific pictures of the sexual abuse of children and I treated her for that, but this is different to this low-level vicarious traumatisation/burnout. It seems like navel gazing on the part of therapists distracting from getting on with the task of helping the client.

MARTINA: It seems generally accepted that vicarious traumatisation needs to be addressed for healthcare professionals working with children.

JILL: It might be 'generally accepted' but does that make it true? I can see that staff, say, working in child protection could reach a point where they want to do something different, but I am not convinced of the usefulness of the term vicarious traumatisation. I have been doing my Master's Dissertation on it and there is a review of the issue by Sabin-Farrell and Turpin (2003) who concluded that 'the evidence to support the existence of vicarious traumatisation is meagre and inconsistent'. I think Dave would have been better off focussing on diagnosis.

The above dialogue illustrates that supervision training not only has to be cognisant of the supervisory process but should emphasise that the content of the supervision session is equally important. In this respect, it reflects the dual focus on content and process when treating depressed clients with CBT. The exchange below indicates that supervisors and trainers may disagree on the number and types of supervisee competences that need to be addressed.

DAVE: I prefer a formulation rather than a diagnosis-based approach.

JILL: But the two are not mutually exclusive.

MARTINA: I don't want us to get lost in the details of different approaches.

LEN: But it makes a difference to the content of the supervision session; are you saying, Martina, that the content doesn't matter?

MARTINA: I don't want to get into that, we could be here all year debating that.

LEN: I come originally from a humanistic background where formulation ruled, then my CBT training taught me that there are different CBT protocols for different disorders, formulation is still about but it is in the form of 'case formulation'.

MARTINA: I'm not sure what you mean by making a difference between formulation and 'case formulation'?

LEN: A formulation is a hypothesis about how the client is functioning, whilst a 'case formulation' is a specific example of the cognitive model of a disorder.

DAVE: My formulation of Gina was her achievements were an overcompensation for feelings of inadequacy stemming from the rape and that if she did less achieving and more connecting she would feel better.

STEPHANIE: But I don't see how that is a CBT approach?

DAVE: CBT is very useful tool, but the work of Norcross, Hogan and Koocher (2008) and Norcross and Wampold (2011) shows that the relationship is more important than the particular type of therapy.

JILL: I don't think that is true. There are too few head-on comparisons of different therapies for different disorders. Lumping all the disorders together and using a non-specific psychometric test to compare the different treatments as Norcross and his colleagues do is nonsense. NICE have looked at the plethora of CBT studies and concluded that pretty well across the spectrum of disorders, diagnosis-based CBT protocols are evidence based.

DAVE: But I do use CBT, thought records, etc.

JILL: It sounds more like CBT flavoured counselling, there is lots of alleged CBT around.

MARTINA: Interesting, but we seem to be getting away from supervision.

STEPHANIE: Actually I think it goes to the heart of the question, what is supervision about? Is it just the processes we talked about at the start of the workshop or is it at least as much about ensuring fidelity to an evidence-based protocol?

The above vignette reflects the diversity of perspectives of supervisors attending a training course and the problems a trainer faces in respecting these differences, ensuring a positive experience for all. These difficulties are compounded when there is disagreement about which supervisee competences should be a focus and how they should be measured. The dialogue continues:

MARTINA: I think it might be useful to continue the role-play and discover whether the differences between us are more apparent/theoretical than real, so I will go back to role-playing if someone else would like to take a turn as supervisor.

JILL: I'll have a go.

MARTINA: Fine.

JILL: What is Gina suffering from?

MARTINA: I think it's depression.

JILL: Anything else?

MARTINA: She might have PTSD from the rape.

JILL: What makes you think it's depression?

MARTINA: On the PHQ9 she scored 24, which is just three short of the maximum.

JILL: Can you be sure that she is really that bad and not just scoring the highest on nearly all the items to make the point she feels really bad?

MARTINA: The only zero was on the item about thoughts she would be better off dead.

JILL: The PHQ9 covers all the symptoms in the DSM IV criteria for depression, you could use it to ask questions about each symptom and to check out whether that symptom is really impairing functioning, doing this approximates to a standardised diagnostic interview which is the most reliable form of assessment. There are stage specific competences (see Chapter 8) which includes Competence in the Initial Evaluation (Table 8.3).

MARTINA: Is that really necessary?

JILL: A Competent Initial Evaluation is an integral part of all the NICE approved CBT protocols. Where is the evidence that it can be jettisoned?

MARTINA: It's a cookbook.

JILL: But the recipe works.

MARTINA: Perhaps I could step out of role and open that exchange for discussion.

DAVE: I think it is appropriate to discuss with a supervisee providing a recording and rating competence on it using the Cognitive Therapy Rating Scale but I don't see why you can't just use that to scrutinise the initial evaluation.

JILL: *The Cognitive Therapy Rating Scale Manual* (Young and Beck, 1980) explicitly states that it is not appropriate for the initial evaluation.

LEN: Without a competent evaluation you will not know whether Gina has PTSD or not from the rape.

DAVE: Come on. It is going to have an effect.

STEPHANIE: It could have had a big effect at the time but might have a minor effect (if any) now, you don't know without a proper evaluation.

JILL: There is no published evidence that PTSD can be reliably diagnosed without using a diagnostic interview.

MARTINA: You used the phrase, Jill, stage-specific competences. What other competence were you including in this?

JILL: I think it is a different ball game when towards the end of therapy, the client has got over their symptoms; assessing such a session with the Cognitive Therapy Rating Scale is inappropriate; the therapist should be assessed using a Relapse Prevention Framework.

LEN: Can the Cognitive Therapy Rating Scale be the litmus test of a therapist, say, midway through therapy the therapist could get good marks on it without following an evidence-based protocol from some unidentified/ignored disorder.

JILL: Yes, there is also a diagnosis specific competence (see Chapter 8), which assesses fidelity to a specific evidence-based CBT protocol and skill in implementing that protocol; thus if Gina had PTSD there would be specific treatment targets and matching treatment strategies, a Sat Nav (Scott, 2009) that the therapist/supervisee should follow.

DAVE: But there are different evidence-based protocols, for the same disorder; it is a bewildering array.

LEN: It doesn't matter which evidence supported treatment (EST) the supervisee goes with, so long as they are not simply responding to the latest crisis in the client's life.

MARTINA: Perhaps I could get into role again and express the reservations I have about all this. OK, Stephanie, if you would you like to play the supervisor.

MARTINA: Following these protocols seems so prescriptive, with all that's going on.

STEPHANIE: I'm sorry. I'm not with you 'with all that is going on?'

MARTINA: I meant at home.

STEPHANIE: At home?

MARTINA: Yes. I have been having an affair. My partner's found out I was going to leave him, he threatened suicide, but the kids love him and I've decided not to leave.

STEPHANIE: Maybe you would like to share all this and then we could look at what it means about work.

MARTINA: I'd like to come out of role here. I certainly felt marking you on the SRQ you were doing really well, acknowledging me and respecting my anxieties but it wasn't prescriptive in the way Jill would have it.

JILL: No, you are creating a caricature of my approach, it is not that I would be prescriptive at each point of every supervision session and I would have responded exactly as Stephanie did but would eventually have addressed why the supervisee's personal chaos meant she was unable to follow a protocol. I'd also have avoided becoming the supervisee's surrogate relationship counsellor.

DAVE: I agree being a supervisee's therapist has no place for a supervisor.

STEPHANIE: I do think allowing the supervisee the opportunity to share is very different to becoming their therapist. I would have thought that following a Sat Nav was going to be actually easier when there is personal chaos.

LEN: I suppose the fear is becoming mechanistic, and talk of a Sat Nav perhaps fans the flames of this.

JILL: I think the mechanistic supervisee is actually a fiction. In all the feedback I've given students and supervisees I can't ever remember commenting that they were mechanistic.

MARTINA: What is the function of the fiction?

LEN: Coming from a humanistic background, there is a great concern to preserve therapist creativity and autonomy. These concerns are still present with many

CBT therapists but I do not believe these are under threat by being faithful to ESTs.

MARTINA: I think what Stephanie showed is that supervision can be still conducted with humanity and fidelity to a CBT approach.

DAVE: *laughing* All this talk of infidelity, makes me think, Stephanie, of yourself and me, what do you think?

LEN: *laughing* No, Dave, we were talking about fidelity, not infidelity.

MARTINA: Now, if Stephanie were your supervisee, Dave, that might be problematic.

STEPHANIE: Tough, Dave, I think that the same ethical principles surround supervisor–supervisee sexual relationships as apply to the therapist–client relationship.

DAVE: No, honestly, I agree with you; sexual relationships in either constitute an unacceptable abuse of power.

The above dialogue illustrates that there are major issues about the appropriate content of supervision that need to be addressed if that supervision is to be part of the professional development of a CBT therapist. But CBT supervision has to conform to the same ethical norms that apply to supervision in general. A regularly occurring problem that CBT supervisors have to address is the issue of complexity/comorbidity and this is addressed in the following vignette:

MARTINA: I would like to go back into the role play, of the supervisee with the client Gina. For the sake of argument let us assume that she is suffering from not only PTSD/depression, but part way through therapy the supervisee discovers that Gina also has a drink problem and he/she brings it up in supervision. I would be intrigued how the supervisor would handle this complexity. Imagine I've just told you this, Len.

LEN: Why didn't you screen drink problem in your initial assessment?

MARTINA: Well, I remember asking her how does drinking fit into your life and Gina said, 'I like a drink after work, always have done'.

LEN: But if you had included a standardised screen for drink problems that is embedded in the First Step Questionnaire [Scott (2009)] you would have picked it up together with whether she wants help with it or not or is ambivalent.

MARTINA: Hmm, not done too good on my stage-specific competence.

LEN: Could be improved.

MARTINA: There's so much to tackle with Gina, drink, PTSD, depression. I don't know where to start.

LEN: What are the options?

MARTINA: Get her admitted for a 3 week detox, then recommence therapy after or just tackle the drink problem first.

LEN: What is the evidence that the drink has to be tackled first and in isolation?

MARTINA: It is standard practise.

LEN: But what is the evidence?

MARTINA: I don't know. Must look into it.

LEN: What is to stop you putting drink, PTSD and depression on the agenda for every session and you address some aspect of the EST for each at each session?

MARTINA: It sounds overwhelming.

LEN: I've not found any problem in doing this, but don't go by me: do the experiment and see what happens.

MARTINA: I would like to stop it there. We do develop therapeutic rules, such as: treat the addiction before any other disorder or complex cases, forget about diagnosis, go by the formulation. A consensus develops and we need to step back and ask whether the rule is evidence-based.

DAVE: That could make for an uncomfortable ride with colleagues.

STEPHANIE: Paradoxically supervision might make life more stressful for the supervisee.

JILL: I think ultimately supervision is about making life better for clients and not necessarily for the supervisee or their employer.

The above dialogue illustrates the importance of a heavy experiential component to the training of supervisors and the practice of supervision but a need to balance it with a focus on the knowledge and competences needed by a supervisee – a dual focus on content and process.

Appendix A

Example supervisor–supervisee contracts

As clinical supervisor, I agree to:

- Meet punctually at regular intervals to offer a minimum of 1 hour and 30 minutes of supervision per week.
- Meet in an environment in which there is as little interruption as possible.
- Maintain confidentiality, which means no information brought up by _____ will be discussed outside the supervisory session apart from:

  1. Within my own supervision (of supervision) where only first names will be revealed.
  2. When there has been a breach of BABCP code of ethics/practice and following discussion with the supervisee it may be necessary to divulge information to other parties (manager, BABCP).

- Treat _____ in a professional manner.
- Keep records of supervision sessions in a secure place – locked filing cabinet in my office.
- Make myself available by telephone between sessions for consultation for urgent matters.
- Adhere to the NMC Code of Conduct, BABCP and UKCP codes of ethics.
- Prepare for supervision sessions.
- Support, encourage and give constructive feedback.
- Challenge practice which is unethical, unwise, insensitive or incompetent.
- Challenge blind spots.
- Review the usefulness of the work done after six months and if necessary re-negotiate the contract.
- Negotiate with _____ when, and if necessary, to make changes to the contract.
- Support _____ in his/her pursuit for BABCP accreditation.

As supervisee, I agree to:

- Meet punctually at regular intervals for a minimum of 1 hour and 30 minutes of supervision per week.
- Maintain confidentiality of clients by using only first names.
- Seek client informed consent if audio recording therapy sessions.

- Consult with _____ by telephone between sessions only when an urgent matter arises.
- Adhere to the BABCP and UKCP code of ethics and NMC code of practice.
- Take responsibility for the work carried out with clients.
- Bring issues to supervision for which consultation is necessary.
- Prepare for supervision sessions and formulate supervision questions.
- Raise difficulties about supervision with _____ when and if these arise.
- Review the usefulness of the work done after six months and if necessary re-negotiate the contract.
- Re-negotiate with _____ when, and if necessary, to make changes or terminate this contract.
- Pursue BABCP accreditation.

Appendix B

Fidelity checklists for Guided Self-Help (GSH) for depression, generalised anxiety disorder, panic disorder and social phobia

Adherence checklist for depression

Did the therapist focus on this and where applicable, its implementation?		
Yes (3), Yes, but insufficiently (2), No (1)		
1	Assess – using CBT Pocketbook, (beginning and end of contact)	
2	Psychoeducation – Section 1 How depression develops and keeps going	
3	Section 2 No investments, no return	
4	Section 3 On second thoughts	
5	Section 4 Just make a start	
6	Section 5 Expectation versus experience and recalling the positive	
7	Section 6 Negative spin or how to make yourself depressed without really trying	
8	Section 7 An attitude problem	
9	Section 8 My attitude to self, others and the future	
10	Section 9 Be critical of your reflex first thoughts not how you feel	
11	Section 10 Preventing relapse	
12	Collaboratively plan homework	
13	Seek feedback on session	
14	Clarify if there are further questions	
15	Agree next appointment	
16	Review homework	

Adherence checklist for generalised anxiety disorder

	Did the therapist focus on this and where applicable, its implementation?	
	Yes (3), Yes, but insufficiently (2), No (1)	
1	Assess – using CBT Pocketbook, (beginning and end of contact)	
2	Psychoeducation – Introduction	
3	Section 1 Worry is controllable	
4	Section 2 Worry is not dangerous	
5	Section 3 Giving up reassurance seeking and blocking of thoughts	
6	Section 4 Worry doesn't work	
7	Section 5 Stop yourself making mountains out of molehills	
8	Section 6 Have realistic expectations	
9	Section7 Accept hassles as inevitable, problem solve them as best you can	
10	Section 8 Use a turnstile rather than have an open door	
11	Section 9 Make realistic predictions, don't get hooked by worst case scenario	
12	Section 10 Practise tolerating uncertainty and anxiety	
13	Section 11 Don't avoid thoughts, greet each thought	
14	Section 12 Dare to live	
15	Section 13 Better managing sleep and irritability	
16	Collaboratively plan homework	
17	Seek feedback on session	
18	Clarify if there are further questions	
19	Agree next appointment	
20	Review homework	

Adherence checklist for panic disorder

	Did the therapist focus on this and where applicable, its implementation?	
	Yes (3), Yes, but insufficiently (2), No (1)	
1	Assess – using CBT Pocketbook, (beginning and end of contact)	
2	Psychoeducation – Introduction	
3	Section 1 Putting a 'danger' label on bodily sensations and using 'safety' procedures guarantees panic	
4	Section 2 If you can think yourself into panic can it be that dangerous?	
5	Section 3 Being on 'sentry duty' for bodily sensations triggers an alarm	
6	Section 4 If you can bring on a panic attack can it be that serious?	
7	Section 5 Slow motion action replay of your most recent bad panic attack and monitoring your attacks	
8	Section 6 Monitoring your avoidance	
9	Section 7 Beginning to dare	
10	Section 8 Saboteurs of the 'dares'	
11	Section 9 Seeing 'dares' as experiments – don't avoid realistic experiments	
12	Section 10 Relapse prevention	
13	Collaboratively plan homework	
14	Seek feedback on session	
15	Clarify if there are further questions	
16	Agree next appointment	
17	Review homework	

Adherence checklist for social phobia

	Did the therapist focus on this and where applicable, its implementation?	
	Yes (3), Yes, but insufficiently (2), No (1)	
I	Assess – using CBT Pocketbook, (beginning and end of contact)	
2	Psychoeducation – Introduction	
3	Section I Beliefs that maintain social anxiety	
4	Section 2 Second thoughts	
5	Section 3 What do others really notice?	
6	Section 4 Daring to drop safety behaviours	
7	Section 5 Checking out whether other people do 'see' what you think they 'see'	
8	Section 6 Revisiting feared situations and what makes a person likeable	
9	Section 7 Haunted by the memory of humiliation – if I knew then what I know now	
10	Section 8 Worry before, during and after a social encounter	
11	Collaboratively plan homework	
12	Seek feedback on session	
13	Clarify if there are further questions	
14	Agree next appointment	
15	Review homework	

Appendix C

Summary of criteria for empirically supported psychological therapies

1   Comparison with a no-treatment control group, alternative treatment group, or placebo (a) in a randomized control trial, controlled single case experiment, or equivalent time-samples design and (b) in which the EST is statistically significantly superior to no treatment, placebo, or alternative treatments or in which the EST is equivalent to a treatment already established in efficacy, and power is sufficient to detect moderate differences.

2   These studies must have been conducted with (a) a treatment manual or its logical equivalent; (b) a population, treated for specified problems, for whom inclusion criteria have been delineated in a reliable, valid manner; (c) reliable and valid outcome assessment measures, at minimum tapping the problems targeted for change; and (d) appropriate data analysis.

3   For a designation of efficacious, the superiority of the EST must have been shown in at least two independent research settings (sample size of three or more at each site in the case of single-case experiments). If there is conflicting evidence, the preponderance of the well-controlled data must support the EST's efficacy.

4   For a designation of possibly efficacious, one study (sample size of three or more in the case of single-case experiments) suffices in the absence of conflicting evidence.

5   For a designation of efficacious and specific, the EST must have been shown to be statistically significantly superior to pill or psychological placebo or to an alternative bona fide treatment in at least two independent research settings. If there is conflicting evidence, the preponderance of the well-controlled data must support the EST's efficacy and specificity.

Appendix D

Treatment adherence scales for depression and the anxiety disorders

Treatment adherence: Depression			
How thoroughly were specific treatment targets and techniques addressed in the session?:			

1 Not done	2	3 Some discussion	4	5 Considerable discussion	6	7 Extensively discussed

Treatment target	Technique	Score
1. Depression about depression	Focus on responsibility for working on solutions and not on responsibility for problem	
2. Inactivity	Developing a broad investment portfolio, wide-ranging modest investments	
3. Negative views of self, personal world and future	Challenging the validity, utility and authority by which these views are held. Use of MOOD chart	
4. Information processing biases	Highlighting personal biases and stepping around them using MOOD chart	
5. Overvalued roles	Valuing multiple roles, renegotiation of roles in social context	
Mean score		

Treatment adherence: Generalised anxiety disorder						
How thoroughly were specific treatment targets and techniques addressed in the session?:						
1 Not done	2	3 Some discussion	4	5 Considerable discussion	6	7 Extensively discussed
Treatment target			Technique			Score
1. Beliefs about the uncontrollability of worry. Beliefs about the danger of worry			Worry postponement, worry time. Planned ignoring of worries			
2. Avoidance, reassurance seeking			Openness to all triggers of worry episodes, trusting in own judgement			
3. Thought control strategies			Demonstration of rebound effect of thought suppression			
4. Positive beliefs about worry			Examination of the evidence and counter evidence			
5. Maladaptive metacognitive beliefs about problem solving and intolerance of uncertainty			Problem orientation and effective problem solving			
6. Task interfering cognitions (TIC), horror video			Switching to task oriented cognitions (TOC) TIC/ TOC. Switching to reality video			
7. Perception that demands exceed resources			Working sequentially rather than simultaneously, weaning off excessive responsibility, responsibility pie			
8. Managing mood			Use of MOOD chart			
9. Tension			Applied relaxation			
Mean score						

Treatment adherence: Obsessive compulsive disorder						
How thoroughly were specific treatment targets and techniques addressed in the session?:						
1 Not done	2	3 Some discussion	4	5 Considerable discussion	6	7 Extensively discussed
Treatment target			Technique			Score
1. Model of mental life, serious misinterpretation of intrusions thought action fusion (TAF), thought object fusion (TOF) and thought event fusion (TEF)			Develop more appropriate model, detached mindfulness about intrusions			
2. Inappropriate goal state, e.g. absolute certainty, perfect cleanliness			Distilling achievable goals			
3. Appraisal of intrusions			Encourage perception of reasonable degree of control by postponement strategies. Use of bOCD chart and completion of Personal Significance Scale			
4. Neutralising images, thoughts, behaviours			Behavioural experiments, Dare Don't Avoid a Realistic Experiment			
5. Overestimation of danger/ intolerance of uncertainty			Distillation of realistic probabilities. The necessity of tolerating uncertainty			
6. Cognitive and behavioural avoidance			Demonstration of the harmlessness of thoughts. Discussion of 'why don't you warn others of these dangers?'			
7. Excessive responsibility, low mood			Responsibility pie, therapist contracts to remove responsibility, MOOD chart, memory aids			
8. Unassertive communication			Communication guidelines			
9. Unrealistic appraisals of the personal significance of intrusions			Challenging appraisals, 'devil's advocate'			
Mean score						

Treatment adherence: Panic disorder						
How thoroughly were specific treatment targets and techniques addressed in the session?:						
1 Not done	2	3 Some discussion	4	5 Considerable discussion	6	7 Extensively discussed
Treatment target			Technique			Score
1. Fear of fear, anxiety sensitivity, catastrophic labelling of bodily symptoms, hypervigilance for bodily symptoms, monitoring of panic attacks			Psychoeducation			
2. Avoidance of activities and situations, anxiety sensitivity			Construction of exposure hierarchy, in vivo and interoceptive exposure			
3. 'Safety' procedures, avoidance			Daring to gradually wean off 'safety' procedures, troubleshooting cognitive saboteurs to continued interoceptive and in vivo exposure			
4. Intolerance of discomfort, feared consequences, key cognitive saboteurs			Interoceptive and in-vivo exposure, challenging 'catastrophic' cognitions, dares as behavioural experiments, downward arrow technique			
Mean score						

Treatment adherence: Posttraumatic stress disorder						
How thoroughly were specific treatment targets and techniques addressed in the session?:						
1 Not done	2	3 Some discussion	4	5 Considerable discussion	6	7 Extensively discussed
Treatment target			Technique			Score
1. Beliefs about PTSD			Normalisation of symptoms, utilisation of Moving On After Trauma			
2. Cognitive and behavioural avoidance			Advantages and disadvantages short and long term of avoidance			
3. 'No one can understand what I've been through'			Realistic portrayal of discomfort to be expected. Underlining similarities of trauma and responses			
4. Managing reminders			The menu of options for handling reminders			
5. Behavioural avoidance. Fear of anxiety			Beginning the journey of a return to normality by gradual 'dares'			
6. Processing of traumatic memory			Written or verbal account of trauma and its effects elaboration of the memory			
7. Motivation			Motivational interviewing			
8. Rumination cognitive avoidance			Disturbed sleep/ nightmares. Addressing the traumatic memory at a specific time and place			
9. Discrimination of triggers			Using similarities and differences			
10. Irritability, emotional avoidance and 'control freak'			Traffic light routine. Managing 'seething' over the trauma and its effects, coping strategies			

11. Persistent and exaggerated negative expectations of oneself, others or the world and persistent distorted blame of self about the cause or consequence of the traumatic event and core maladaptive schemas in PTSD	Use of MOOD chart to modify observed thinking and underlying assumptions. Use of magnifying glass analogy to illustrate exaggeratedly negative view of self, others and world	
12. Cognitive avoidance Behavioural avoidance Hypervigilance for danger	Attention control and detached mindfulness. Continuing to 'dare'	
13. Impaired relationships	Beginning to invest in people	
14. Low mood, pain/disability View of self, world and future	Mood management strategies. Cognitive restructuring, the importance of a broad investment portfolio	
Mean score		

Treatment adherence: Social phobia		
How thoroughly were specific treatment targets and techniques addressed in the session?:		

1 Not done	2	3 Some discussion	4	5 Considerable discussion	6	7 Extensively discussed

Treatment target	Technique	Score
1. 'I'm an oddity'. Beliefs that maintain social anxiety	Distillation of working model of disorder. Questioning of typical thoughts (on 'second thoughts'). Survey to determine what makes people 'acceptable'	
2. 'Inside' view of self. Expectation of high standards	Contrasting 'Inside' view of self with 'Outside' view of others using video feedback. Exposure to feared situations. Survey to determine standards of others	
3. Safety behaviours. Information processing biases	Contrasting anxiety experienced using safety behaviours with those when not using. Vigilance for all or nothing thinking, personalisation, mind-reading and mental filter	
4. Non-disclosure of personal information	Modelling and role play of selfdisclosure	
5. Anticipatory anxiety and postevent rumination. Past humiliations	Cognitive restructuring and rescripting	
6. Anticipatory anxiety and postevent rumination	Moderating worry and disengagement from it	
Mean score		

Appendix E

Treatment fidelity scales for depression and the anxiety disorders

Treatment adherence and competence: Depression							Competence: How skilfully was the target addressed using the particular techniques? Rate 1-7, where 1 is no competence and 7 is total competence
Adherence: How thoroughly were specific treatment targets and techniques addressed in the session?:							
1 Not done	2	3 Some discussion	4	5 Considerable discussion	6	7 Extensively discussed	
Treatment target			Technique			Score	
1. Depression about depression			Focus on responsibility for working on solutions and not on responsibility for problem				
2. Inactivity			Developing a broad investment portfolio, wide-ranging modest investments				
3. Negative views of self, personal world and future			Challenging the validity, utility and authority by which these views are held. Use of MOOD chart				
4. Information processing biases			Highlighting personal biases and stepping around them using MOOD chart				

5. Overvalued roles	Valuing multiple roles, renegotiation of roles in social context		
Mean score			

Treatment Fidelity: Generalised anxiety disorder							Competence: How skilfully was the target addressed using the particular techniques? Rate 1-7, where 1 is no competence and 7 is total competence
Adherence: How thoroughly were specific treatment targets and techniques addressed in the session?:							
1 Not done	2	3 Some discussion	4	5 Considerable discussion	6	7 Extensively discussed	
Treatment target			Technique			Score	
1. Beliefs about the uncontrollability of worry. Beliefs about the danger of worry			Worry postponement, worry time. Planned ignoring of worries				
2. Avoidance, reassurance seeking			Openness to all triggers of worry episodes, trusting in own judgement				
3. Thought control strategies			Demonstration of rebound effect of thought suppression				
4. Positive beliefs about worry			Examination of the evidence and counter evidence				
5. Maladaptive metacognitive beliefs about problem solving and intolerance of uncertainty			Problem orientation and effective problem solving				

6. Task interfering cognitions (TIC), horror video	Switching to task oriented cognitions (TOC) TIC/TOC Switching to reality video		
7. Perception that demands exceed resources	Working sequentially rather than simultaneously, weaning off excessive responsibility, responsibility pie		
8. Managing mood	Use of MOOD chart		
9. Tension	Applied relaxation		
Mean score			

Treatment fidelity: Obsessive compulsive disorder			
Adherence: How thoroughly were specific treatment targets and techniques addressed in the session?:			Competence: How skilfully was the target addressed using the particular techniques? Rate 1-7, where 1 is no competence and 7 is total competence

1 Not done	2	3 Some discussion	4	5 Considerable discussion	6	7 Extensively discussed	

Treatment target	Technique	Score	
1. Model of mental life, serious misinterpretation of intrusions thought action fusion (TAF), thought object fusion (TOF) and thought event fusion (TEF)	Develop more appropriate model, detached mindfulness about intrusions		

2. Inappropriate goal state, e.g. absolute certainty, perfect cleanliness	Distilling achievable goals		
3. Appraisal of intrusions	Encourage perception of reasonable degree of control by postponement strategies. Use of bOCD chart and completion of Personal Significance Scale		
4. Neutralising images, thoughts, behaviours	Behavioural experiments, Dare – Don't Avoid a Realistic Experiment		
5. Overestimation of danger/intolerance of uncertainty	Distillation of realistic probabilities. The necessity of tolerating uncertainty		
6. Cognitive and behavioural avoidance	Demonstration of the harmlessness of thoughts. Discussion of 'why don't you warn others of these dangers?'		
7. Excessive responsibility, low mood	Responsibility pie, therapist contracts to remove responsibility, MOOD chart, memory aids		
8. Unassertive communication	Communication guidelines		
9. Unrealistic appraisals of the personal significance of intrusions	Challenging appraisals, 'devil's advocate'		
Mean score			

Treatment fidelity: Panic disorder	
Adherence: How thoroughly were specific treatment targets and techniques addressed in the session?:	Competence: How skilfully was the target addressed using the particular techniques? Rate 1-7, where 1 is no competence and 7 is total competence

1 Not done	2	3 Some discussion	4	5 Considerable discussion	6	7 Extensively discussed	

Treatment target	Technique	Score	
1. Fear of fear, anxiety sensitivity, catastrophic labelling of bodily symptoms, hypervigilance for bodily symptoms, monitoring of panic attacks	Psychoeducation		
2. Avoidance of activities and situations, anxiety sensitivity	Construction of exposure hierarchy, in vivo and interoceptive exposure		
3. 'Safety' procedures, avoidance	Daring to gradually wean off 'safety' procedures, troubleshooting cognitive saboteurs to continued interoceptive and in vivo exposure		
4. Intolerance of discomfort, feared consequences, key cognitive saboteurs	Interoceptive and in-vivo exposure, challenging 'catastrophic' cognitions, dares as behavioural experiments, downward arrow technique		
Mean score			

Treatment fidelity: Posttraumatic stress disorder			
Adherence: How thoroughly were specific treatment targets and techniques addressed in the session?:			*Competence: How skilfully was the target addressed using the particular techniques? Rate 1-7, where 1 is no competence and 7 is total competence*
1 Not done 2 3 Some discussion	4 5 Considerable discussion	6 7 Extensively discussed	
Treatment target	Technique	Score	
1. Beliefs about PTSD	Normalisation of symptoms utilisation of Moving On After Trauma		
2. Cognitive and behavioural avoidance	Advantages and disadvantages short and long term of avoidance		
3. 'No one can understand what I've been through'	Realistic portrayal of discomfort to be expected. Underlining similarities of trauma and responses		
4. Managing reminders	The menu of options for handling reminders		
5. Behavioural avoidance. Fear of anxiety	Beginning the journey of a return to normality by gradual 'dares'		
6. Processing of traumatic memory	Written or verbal account of trauma and its effects elaboration of the memory		

7. Motivation	Motivational interviewing		
8. Rumination Cognitive avoidance	Disturbed sleep/ nightmares. Addressing the traumatic memory at a specific time and place		
9. Discrimination of triggers	Using similarities and differences		
10. Irritability, emotional avoidance and 'control freak'	Traffic light routine. Managing 'seething' over the trauma and its effects, coping strategies		
11. Persistent and exaggerated negative expectations of oneself, others or the world and persistent distorted blame of self about the cause or consequence of the traumatic event and core maladaptive schemas in PTSD	Use of MOOD chart to modify observed thinking and underlying assumptions. Use of magnifying glass analogy to illustrate exaggeratedly negative view of self, others and world		
12. Cognitive avoidance Behavioural avoidance Hypervigilance for danger	Attention control and detached mindfulness. Continuing to 'dare'		
13. Impaired relationships	Beginning to invest in people		
14. Low mood, pain/ disability View of self, world and future	Mood management strategies. Cognitive restructuring, the importance of a broad investment portfolio		
Mean score			

Treatment fidelity: Social phobia							
Adherence: How thoroughly were specific treatment targets and techniques addressed in the session?:							*Competence: How skilfully was the target addressed using the particular techniques? Rate 1-7, where 1 is no competence and 7 is total competence*
1 Not done	2	3 Some discussion	4	5 Considerable discussion	6	7 Extensively discussed	
Treatment target		Technique		Score			
1. 'I'm an oddity'. Beliefs that maintain social anxiety		Distillation of working model of disorder. Questioning of typical thoughts (on 'second thoughts'). Survey to determine what makes people 'acceptable'					
2. 'Inside' view of self. Expectation of high standards		Contrasting 'Inside' view of self with 'Outside' view of others using video feedback. Exposure to feared situations. Survey to determine standards of others					
3. Safety behaviours. Information processing biases		Contrasting anxiety experienced using safety behaviours with those when not using. Vigilance for all or nothing thinking, personalisation, mind-reading and mental filter					
4. Non-disclosure of personal information		Modelling and role play of self-disclosure					

5. Anticipatory anxiety and post-event rumination. Past humiliations	Cognitive restructuring and rescripting		
6. Anticipatory anxiety and post-event rumination	Moderating worry and disengagement from it		
Mean score			

Appendix F

The Supervisory Relationship Questionnaire (SRQ)

The following statements describe some of the ways a person may feel about his/her supervisor. To what extent do you agree or disagree with each of the following statements about your relationship with your supervisor? Please tick the column which matches your opinion most closely.	Strongly Disagree	Disagree	Slightly Disagree	Neither Agree nor Disagree	Slightly Agree	Agree	Strongly Agree
SAFE BASE SUBSCALE							
1. My supervisor was respectful of my views and ideas							
2. My supervisor and I were equal partners in supervision							
3. My supervisor had a collaborative approach in supervision							
4. I felt safe in my supervision sessions							
5. My supervisor was non-judgemental in supervision							
6. My supervisor treated me with respect							
7. My supervisor was open-minded in supervision							

8. Feedback on my performance from my supervisor felt like criticism							
9. The advice I received from my supervisor was prescriptive rather than collaborative							
10. I felt able to discuss my concerns with my supervisor openly							
11. Supervision felt like an exchange of ideas							
12. My supervisor gave feedback in a way that felt safe							
13. My supervisor treated me like an adult							
14. I was able to be open with my supervisor							
15. I felt if I discussed my feelings openly with my supervisor, I would be negatively evaluated							
STRUCTURE SUBSCALE							
16. My supervision sessions took place regularly							
17. Supervision sessions were structured							
18. My supervisor made sure that our supervision sessions were kept free from interruptions							
19. Supervision sessions were regularly cut short by my supervisor							
20. Supervision sessions were focused							
21. My supervision sessions were disorganised							

22. My supervision sessions were arranged in advance							
23. My supervisor and I both drew up an agenda for supervision together							

COMMITMENT SUBSCALE

24. My supervisor was enthusiastic about supervising me							
25. My supervisor appeared interested in supervising me							
26. My supervisor appeared uninterested in me							
27. My supervisor appeared interested in me as a person							
28. My supervisor appeared to like supervising							
29. I felt like a burden to my supervisor							
30. My supervisor was approachable							
31. My supervisor was available to me							
32. My supervisor paid attention to my spoken feelings and anxieties							
33. My supervisor appeared interested in my development as a professional							

REFLECTIVE EDUCATION SUBSCALE

34. My supervisor drew from a number of theoretical models							
35. My supervisor drew from a number of theoretical models flexibly							
36. My supervisor gave me the opportunity to learn about a range of models							

37. My supervisor encouraged me to reflect on my practice							
38. My supervisor linked theory and clinical practice well							
39. My supervisor paid close attention to the process of supervision							
40. My supervisor acknowledged the power differential between supervisor and supervisee							
41. My relationship with my supervisor allowed me to learn by experimenting with different therapeutic techniques							
42. My supervisor paid attention to my unspoken feelings and anxieties							
43. My supervisor facilitated interesting and informative discussions in supervision							
44. I learnt a great deal from observing my supervisor							
ROLE MODEL SUBSCALE							
45. My supervisor was knowledgeable							
46. My supervisor was an experienced clinician							
47. I respected my supervisor's skills							
48. My supervisor was knowledgeable about the organisational system in which they worked							
49. Colleagues appeared to respect my supervisor's views							
50. I respected my supervisor as a professional							

51. My supervisor gave me practical support							
52. I respected my supervisor as a clinician							
53. My supervisor was respectful of clients							
54. I respected my supervisor as a person							
55. My supervisor appeared uninterested in his / her clients							
56. My supervisor treated his / her colleagues with respect							
FORMATIVE FEEDBACK SUBSCALE							
57. My supervisor gave me helpful negative feedback on my performance							
58. My supervisor was able to balance negative feedback on my performance with praise							
59. My supervisor gave me positive feedback on my performance							
60. My supervisor's feedback on my performance was constructive							
61. My supervisor paid attention to my level of competence							
62. My supervisor helped me identify my own learning needs							
63. My supervisor did not consider the impact of my previous skills and experience on my learning needs							
64. My supervisor thought about my training needs							

65. My supervisor gave me regular feedback on my performance							
66. As my skills and confidence grew, my supervisor adapted supervision to take this into account							
67. My supervisor tailored supervision to my level of competence							

Scoring Key

Unshaded items scored 1 (Strongly Disagree) to 7 (Strongly Agree).

Reverse Scoring

Shaded items scored 7 (Strongly Disagree) to 1 (Strongly Agree).

Source: Palomo, Beinart and Cooper (2010).

References

Aaarons, G. A., Sommerfield, D. H., Hecht, D. B., Silovsky, J. F. and Chaffin, M. J. (2009). The impact of evidence-based practice implementation and fidelity monitoring on staff turnover: Evidence for a protective effect. *Journal of Consulting and Clinical Psychology*, 77, 270–80.

Achenbach, T. M. (2005). Advancing assessment of children and adolescents: Commentary on evidence-based assessment of child and adolescent disorders. *Journal of Clinical Child and Adolescent Psychology*, 34, 541–7.

Addis, M. and Krasnow, A. (2000). A national survey of practicing psychologists' attitudes toward psychotherapy treatment manuals. *Consulting and Clinical Psychology* 68, 331–9.

Addis, M., Wade, W. and Hatgis, C. (1999). Barriers to dissemination of evidence-based practices: Addressing practitioners' concerns about manual-based psychotherapies. *Clinical Psychology Science and Practice* 6, 430–41.

Alford, B. A. and Beck, A. T. (1997). *The Integrative Power of Cognitive Therapy*. New York: Guilford Press.

Arch, J. J., Eifert, G. H., Davies, C., Vilardga, J. C. P., Rose, R. D. and Craske, M. G. (2012). Randomized clinical trial of cognitive behavioural therapy (CBT) versus Acceptance and Commitment Therapy (ACT) for mixed anxiety disorders. *Journal of Consulting and Clinical Psychology*, Advance online publication. DOI: 10.1037/a0028310.

Attkisson, C. C. and Zwick, R. (1982). The client satisfaction questionnaire: Psychometric properties and correlations with service utilisation and psychotherapy outcome. *Evaluation Program Planning*, 5, 233–7.

Bambling, M., King, R., Raue, P., Schweitzer, R. and Lambert, W. (2006). Clinical supervision: Its influence on client-rated working alliance and client symptom reduction in the brief treatment of major depression. *Psychotherapy Research*, 16, 317–31.

Basco, M. R., Bostic, J. Q., Davies, D., Rush, A. J., Witte, B., Hendrickse, W. and Barnett, V. (2000). Methods to improve diagnostic accuracy in a community mental health setting. *American Journal of Psychiatry*, 157, 1599–605.

Beach, S. R. H. and O'Leary, K. D. (1986). The treatment of depression in the context of marital discord. *Behaviour Therapy*, 17, 43–9.

Beck, A. T. and Freeman, A. T. (1990). *Cognitive Therapy of Personality Disorders*. New York: Guilford Press.

Beck, A. T., Freeman, A. and Davis, D. (2007). *Cognitive Therapy of Personality Disorders* 2nd Edition. New York: Guilford Press.

Beck, A. T. and Hurvich, M. S. (1959). Psychological correlates of depression: 1. Frequency of 'masochistic' dream content in a private practice sample. *Psychosomatic Medicine*, 21(1), 50–5.

Beck, A. T., Ward, C. H., Mendelson, M., Mock, J. E. and Erbaugh, J. K. (1962). Reliability of psychiatrics diagnoses: A study of consistency of clinical judgements and ratings. *American Journal of Psychiatry*, 119, 351–7.

Beck, A. T., Rush, A. J., Shaw, B. and Emery, G. (1979). *Cognitive Therapy of Depression*. New York: Guilford.

Benjamin, L. T. and Baker, D. B. (Eds) (2000). History of Psychology: The Boulder Conference. *American Psychologist*, 55, 233–54.

Bilsker, D. and Goldner, E. M. (1999). Teaching evidence-based practice in mental health. *Evidence-Based Mental Health*, 2, 68–9.

Blackburn, I. M., James, I. A., Milne, D. L., Baker, C., Standart, S., Garland, A. and Reichelt, F. K. (2001). The revised cognitive therapy scale (CTS-R): Psychometric properties. *Behavioural and Cognitive Psychotherapy*, 29, 431–46.

Blake, D., Weather, F., Nogy, K., Kaloupek, D., Klauminzer, G., Charney, D. and Keane, D. (1990). A clinician rating scale for assessing current and lifetime PTSD: The CAS-1. *Behavior Therapist*, 13, 187–8.

Bowden-Jones, H. and Smith, N. (2012). The medical management of problem gamblers. *British Medical Journal*, 344, 10.

Bradshaw, T., Butterworth, A. and Mairs, H. (2007). Does structured clinical supervision during psychosocial intervention education enhance outcome for mental health nurses and the service users they work with? *Journal of Psychiatric and Mental Health Nursing*, 14, 4–12.

Brown, G. K., Have, T. T., Henriques, G. R., Xie, S. X., Hollander, J. E. and Beck, A. T. (2005). Cognitive therapy for the prevention of suicide attempts: a randomized control trial. *Journal of the American Medical Association*, 294, 563–70.

Brown, J. S. L., Sellwood, K., Beecham, J. K., Slade, M., Andiappan, M., Landau, S., Johnson, T. and Smith, R. (2011). Outcome, costs, and patient engagement for group and individual CBT for depression: A naturalistic clinical study. *Behavioural and Cognitive Psychotherapy*, 39, 355–8.

Bruchmuller, K., Margraf, J., Suppiger, A. and Schneider, S. (2011). Popular or unpopular? Therapists' use of structured interviews and their estimation of patient acceptance. *Behavior Therapy*, 42, 634–43.

Burns, D. (1999) *Feeling Good: The New Mood Therapy*. New York: Avon Books.

Butler, A. C., Chapman, J. E., Forman, E. M. and Beck, A. T. (2006) The empirical status of cognitive-behavioral therapy: A review of meta-analyses. *Clinical Psychology Review*, 26, 17–31.

Carpenter, J., Webb, C., Bostock, L. and Coomber, C. (2012). Effective supervision in social work and social care. *Social Care Institute for Excellence* (SCIE), www.scie.org.uk/publications

Cella, M., Stahl, D., Reme, S. E. and Chalder, T. (2011). Therapist effects in routine psychotherapy practice: an account from chronic fatigue syndrome. *Psychotherapy Research*, 21, 168–78.

Chambless, D. L. and Hollon, S. D. (1998). Defining empirically supported therapies. *Journal of Consulting and Clinical Psychology*, 66, 7–18.

Cheavens, J. S., Strunk, D. R., Lazarus, S. A. and Goldstein, L. A. (2012). The compensation and capitalization models: A test of two approaches to individualizing the treatment of depression, *Behaviour Research and Therapy*, 50, 699–706.

Chevron, E. and Rounsaville, B. J. (1983). Evaluating the clinical skills of psychotherapists: A comparison of techniques. *Archives of General Psychiatry*, 40, 1129–32.

Cook, J. M., Weingardt, K. R., Jaszka, J. and Wiesner, M. (2008). A content analysis of advertisements for psychotherapy workshops: Implications for disseminating empirically supported treatments. *Journal of Clinical Psychology*, 64(3), 296–307.

Coull, G. and Morriss, P. G. (2011). The clinical effectiveness of CBT-based guided self-help interventions for anxiety and depressive disorders: A systematic review. *Psychological Medicine*, 2239–52.

DiGiuseppe, R. and Tafrate, R. (2003). Anger treatment for adults: A meta-analysis review. *Clin Psychol Sci Pract* 10, 70–48.

Eccleston, C., Williams, A. C. and Morley, S. (2009). Review: Limited evidence that psychological therapies are of benefit for adults with chronic pain, *Evidence-based Mental Health*, 12, 118.

Ellis, A. (1962). *Reason and Emotion in Psychotherapy*. Secaucus, NJ: Citadel Press.

Emmelkamp, P. M. G., Benner, A., Kuipers, A., Feiertag, G. A., Koster, H. C. and Van Apeldorn, F. J. (2006). Comparison of brief dynamic and cognitive behavioural therapies in avoidant personality disorder *British Journal of Psychiatry* (2006), 189, 60–4.

Eyberg, S. M. and Ross, A. W. (1978). Assessment of child behaviour problems: The validation of a new inventory. *Journal of Clinical Child Psychology*, 12, 347–54.

Feigenbaum, J. D., Fonagy, P., Pilling, S., Jones, A., Wildgoose, A. and Bebbington, P. E. (2012). A real-world study of the effectiveness of DBT in the UK National Health Service. *British Journal of Clinical Psychology*, 51, 121–41.

Fennell, M. (1999). *Overcoming low self-esteem: Self-help guide using Cognitive behavioural Techniques*. London: Robinson Publishing.

First, M. B., Spitzer, R. L., Gibbon, M. and Williams, J. B. W. (1997a). *Structured Clinical Interview for DSM IV Axis 1 Disorders – Clinician Version* (SCID-CV). Washington, DC: American Psychiatric Press.

Gallo, K. and Barlow, D. H. (2012). Factors involved in clinical adoption and non-adoption of evidence-based interventions in mental health. *Clinical Psychology Science and Practice*, 19, 93–106.

Galovski, T. E., Blain, L. M., Mott, J. M., Elwood, L. and Houle, T. (2012). Manualized therapy for PTSD: Flexing the structure of cognitive processing therapy, *Journal of Consulting and Clinical Psychology*, 80, 968–81.

Gibbons, C. J., Fournier, J. C., Stirman, S. W., DeRubeis, R. J., Crits-Christoph, P. and Beck, A. T. (2010) The clinical effectiveness of cognitive therapy for depression in an outpatient clinic. *Journal of Affective Disorders*, 125, 169–76.

Ginzburg, D. M., Bohn, C., Hofling, V., Weck, F., Clark, D. M. and Stangier, U. (2012). Treatment specific competence predicts outcome in cognitive therapy for social anxiety disorder. *Behaviour Research and Therapy*, 50, 747–52.

Gordon, P. K. (2012). Ten steps to cognitive behavioural supervision, *The Cognitive Behaviour Therapist*, x, 1–12

Grant, A., Townend, M., Mills, J. and Cockx, A. (2008). *Assessment and Case Formulation in Cognitive Behavioural Therapy*. London: Sage Publications.

Grove, W. N., Zald, D. H., Lebow, B. S., Snitz, B. E. and Nelson, C. (2000). Clinical versus mechanical prediction: A meta-analysis. *Psychological Assessment*, 12, 19–30.

Hayes, S. C., Strosahl, K. D. and Wilson, K. G. (1999). *Acceptance and Commitment Therapy: An experiential approach to behavior change*. New York: Guilford Press.

Herschell, A. D., Kolko, D. J., Baumann, B. L. and Davis, A. C. (2010). The role of thera-pist training in the implementation of psychosocial treatments: A review and critique with recommendations. *Clinical Psychology Review*, 30, 448–66.

Hofman, S. G. and Smits, J. A. J. (2008). Cognitive-behavioral therapy for adult anxiety disorders: A meta-analysis of randomised placebo-controlled trials. *Journal of Clinical Psychiatry*, 69, 621–32.

Hooley, J. M., Orley, J. and Teasdale, J. D. (1986). Levels of expressed emotion and relapse in depressed patients. *British Journal of Psychiatry*, 148, 642–7.

Huppert, J. D., Bufka, L. F., Barlow, D. H., Gorman, J. M., Shear, M. K. and Woods, S. W. (2001). Therapists, therapist variables and cognitive-behavioral therapy outcome in a multicentre trial for panic disorder. *Journal of Consulting and Clinical Psychology*, 69, 747–55.

IAPT. (2008). *National Guidelines for Regional Delivery Improving Access to Psychological Therapies: Implementation plan: Curriculum for high-intensity workers.* Department of Health Mental Health Programme.

Jacobson, N. S. and Gortner, E. T. (2000). Can depression be de-medicalised in the 21st century: Scientific revolutions, counter revolutions and the magnetic field of normal science. *Behaviour Research and Therapy*, 38, 103–17.

Kahneman, D., Slovic, P. and Tversky, A. (1982). *Judgement Under Uncertainty: Heuristics and Biases.* New York: Cambridge University Press.

Kahneman, D. (2011). *Thinking, Fast and Slow.* London: Allen Lane

Kazantis, N., Deane, F. P. and Ronan, K. R. (2000). Homework assignments in cognitive and behavioural therapy: A meta-analysis. *Clinical Psychology: Science and Practice*, 7, 189–202.

Kazdin, A. E. (2008). Evidence-based treatment and practice: New opportunities to bridge clinical research and practice, enhance the knowledge base, and improve patient care. *American Psychologist*, 63(3), 146–59.

——. (2011). Evidence-based treatment research: Advances, limitations, and next steps. *American Psychologist*, November, 685–98.

Keller, M. B., Lavori, P., Mueller, T. and Endicott, J. (1992). Time to recovery, chronicity and levels of psychopathology in major depression. A 5-year prospective follow-up of 431 subjects. *Archives of General Psychiatry*, 49, 809–16.

Kendall, P., Gosch, E., Furr, J. and Sood, E. (2008). Flexibility within fidelity. *Journal of the American Academy of Child and Adolescent Psychiatry*, 47, 987–93.

Kendall, P. C. and Hedtke, K. (2006). *Cognitive-Behavioral Therapy for Anxious Children: Therapist manual.* 3rd edition. Ardmore, PA: Workbook Publishing.

Kendall, P. C., Settipani, C. A. and Cummings, C. M. (2012). No need to worry: The prom-ising future of child anxiety research, *Journal of Clinical Child and Adolescent Psychology*, 41(1), 103–15.

Kinderman, P., Read, J., Moncrief, J. and Bentall, R. P. (2013). Drop the language of disorder. *Evidence Based Mental Health*, 16, 2–3.

Kolb, D. A. (1984). *Experiential Learning Experience as the Source of Learning and Development.* Englewood Cliffs, NJ: Prentice Hall.

Kroenke, K., Spitzer, R. L. and Williams, J. B. (2001). The PHQ-9: Validity of a brief depression measure. *Journal of General Internal Medicine*, 16, 606–13.

Kuyken, W., Fothergill, C. D., Musa, M. and Chadwick, P. (2005). The reliability and quality of cognitive case formulation. *Behaviour Research and Therapy*, 43, 1187–201.

Kuyken, W. (2006). 'Evidence-based case formulation: Is the emperor clothed'. In *Case Formulation in Cognitive Behaviour Therapy: The treatment of challenging and complex cases*, N. Tarrier (ed.). London: Routledge.

Kuyken, W. and Tsivrikos, D. (2009). Therapist competence, comorbidity and cognitive-behavioral therapy for depression. *Psychotherapy and Psychosomatics*, 78, 42–8.

Lewis, C. A., Simons, A. D and Kim, H. K. (2012). The role of early symptom trajectories and pre-treatment variables in predicting treatment response to cognitive behavioural therapy. *Journal of Consulting and Clinical Psychology*, 80(4), 525–34.

Lewis, K. (2012). Update on Supervision developments in Behavioural and Cognitive Psychotherapies – a Personal View, issued with Volume 40, Issue 1 of *CBT Today*.

Linehan, M. (1993) *Cognitive-behavioral Treatment of Borderline Personality Disorder*. New York: Guilford Press.

Lovell, K. and Richards, D. A. (2007). *A Recovery Programme for Depression*. London: Rethink.

Lovell, K., Bower, P., Richards, D., Barkham, M., Sibbald, B., Roberts, C., Davies, L., Rogers, A., Gellatly, J. and Hennessy, S. (2008). Developing guided self-help for depression using the Medical Research Council complex interventions framework: A description of the modelling phase and results of an exploratory randomised controlled trial. *BMC Psychiatry*, 8, 91.

McManus, S., Howard Meltzer, H., Brugha, T., Bebbington, P. and Jenkins, R. (2009). *Adult Psychiatric Morbidity in England, 2007: Results of a household survey*. London: The Health and Social Care Information Centre.

McManus, F., Rakovshik, S., Kennerley, H., Fennell, M. and Westbrook, D. (2012). An investigation of the accuracy of therapist's self-assessment of cognitive-behaviour therapy skills. *British Journal of Clinical Psychology*, 51, 292–306.

Makhinson, M. (2012). Biases in the evaluation of psychiatric clinical evidence. *Journal of Nervous and Mental Disease*, 200, 76–82.

Martell, C. R., Dimidjian, S. and Herman-Dunn, R. (2010). *Behavioral Activation for Depression: A clinician's guide*. New York: Guilford Press.

Mausbach, B. T., Moore, R., Roesch, S., Cardenas, V. and Patterson, T. L. (2010). The relationship between homework compliance and therapy outcomes: An updated meta-analysis. *Cognitive Therapy and Research*, 34, 429–38.

Meichenbaum, D. (1985). *Stress Inoculation Training*. London: Pergamon Press.

Meiser-Stedman, R., Smith, P., Bryant, R., Salmon, K., Yule, W., Dalgleish, T. and Nixon, R. D. V. (2009). Development and validation of the child post-traumatic cognitions inventory (CPTCI). *Journal of Child Psychology and Psychiatry*, 50, 432–40.

Mercier, H. and Sperber, D. (2011) Why do humans reason? Arguments for an argumentative theory. *Behavioral and Brain Sciences*, 34, 57–111.

Miller, P. R. (2002). Inpatient diagnostic assessments: 3. Causes and effects on diagnostic imprecision. *Psychiatry Research*, 111, 191–7.

Milne, D. L (2008). CBT Supervision: From reflexivity to specialization. *Behavioural and Cognitive Psychotherapy* 36, 779–86.

Milne, D. L., Sheikh A. I., Pattison, S. and Wilkinson, A. (2011). Evidence-based training for clinical supervisors: A systematic review of 11 controlled studies. *The Clinical Supervisor* 30, 53–71.

Morley, S., Eccleston, C. and Williams, A. (2000). Review: cognitive and behaviour therapies are effective for chronic pain. *Evidence-based Mental Health*, 3, 22.

Morrison, A. P., French, P. and Stewart S. L. K. (2012). Early detection and intervention evaluation for people at risk of psychosis: Multisite randomised controlled trial. *British Medical Journal*, 5 April. 344: e2233. DOI: 10.1136/bmj.e2233.

Muslin, H. L., Thumblad, R. J. and Meschel, G. (1981). The fate of the clinical interview: An observational study. *American Journal of Psychiatry*, 138, 822–5.

Najman, J. M., Williams, G. M., Nikles, J., Spence, S., Bor, W., O'Callaghan, M., Le Brocque, R. and Andersen, M. J. (2000). Mother's mental illness and child behaviour problems: Cause-effect association or observation bias? *Journal of the American Academy of Child and Adolescent Psychiatry*, 39, 592–602.

Nezu, A. M. and Nezu, C. M. (1989). *Problem-solving Therapy for Depression: Theory research and clinical guidelines*. New York: John Wiley & Sons.

Nezu, A. M. and Perri, M. G. (1989). Problem-solving therapy for unipolar depression: An initial dismantling investigation. *Journal of Consulting and Clinical Psychology*, 57, 408–13.

Nezu, A. M., Nezu, C. M. and Lombardo, E. (2004). *Cognitive-behavioral Case-formulation and Treatment Design*. New York: Springer Publishing Company.

Norcross, J. C., Hogan, T. P. and Koocher, G. P. (2008). *Clinician's Guide to Evidence-based Practices: Mental health and the addictions*. New York: Oxford University Press.

Norcross, J. C. and Wampold, B. E. (2011). Evidence-based therapy relationships: Research conclusions and clinical practices. *Psychotherapy*, 48, 98–102.

Norton, P. J. and Barrera, T. L. (2012). Transdiagnostic versus diagnosis-specific CBT for anxiety disorders: A preliminary randomized controlled non-inferiority trial. *Depression and Anxiety*, 29, 874–82.

Oei, T. P. S. and Boschen, M. J. (2009). Clinical effectiveness of a cognitive behavioural group treatment program for anxiety disorders: A benchmark study. *Journal of Anxiety Disorders*, 23, 950–7.

Overholser, J. C. (2011). Collaborative empiricism, guided discovery and the Socratic method: Core processes for effective cognitive therapy. *Clinical Psychology: Science and Practice*, 18, 62–6.

Padesky, C. (1996). Developing cognitive therapist competency: Teaching and supervision Models. In Salkovskis, P. M. (ed.) *Frontiers of Cognitive Therapy*, pp. 266–92. London: Guilford.

Palomo, M., Beinart, H. and Cooper, M. (2010). Development and validation of the, supervisory Relationship Questionnaire (SRQ) in UK trainee clinical psychologists. *British Journal of Clinical Psychology*, 49, 131–49.

Panagioti, M., Gooding, P. A. and Tarrier, N. (2012). A meta-analysis of the association between post-traumatic stress disorder and suicidality: The role of comorbid depression. *Comprehensive Psychiatry*, 53, 915–30.

Persons, J. (2006). Naturalistic outcome of case formulation-driven cognitive-behavior therapy for anxious depressed outpatients. *Behaviour Research and Therapy*, 44, 1041–51.

Petty, R. E. and Cacioppo, J. T. (1986). The elaboration likelihood model of persuasion, *Adavances in Experimental and Social Psychology*, 19, 123–205.

Price, J. R., Mitchell, E., Tidy, E. and Hunot, V. (2008). *Cognitive behaviour therapy for chronic fatigue syndrome in adults* (Review). The Cochrane Library.

Resick, P. A., Nishith, P., Weaver, T. L., Astin, M. C. and Feur, C. A. (2002). A comparison of cognitive-processing therapy with prolonged exposure and a waiting condition for the victims of chronic posttraumatic stress disorder in female rape victims, *Journal of Consulting and Clinical Psychology*, 70, 867–979.

Reynolds, S., Wilson, C., Austin, J. and Hooper, L. (2012). Effects of psychotherapy for anxiety in children and adolescents: A meta-nalytic review. *Clinical Psychology Review*, 32, 251–62.

Richards, D. A. and Borglin, G. (2011). Implementation of psychological therapies for anxiety and depression in routine practice: Two year prospective study. *Journal of Affective Disorders*, 133, 51–60.

Rogers, E. M. (2003). *Diffusion of Innovations* 5th edition. New York: Free Press.

Rollinson, R., Smith, B., Steel, C., Jolley, S., Onwumere, J., Garety, P. A., Kuipers, E., Freeman, D., Bebbington, P. E., Dunn, G., Startup, M. and Fowler, D. (2008). Messuring adherence in CBT for psychosis: A psychometric analysis of an adherence scale. *Behavioural and Cognitive Psychotherapy*, 36, 163–78.

Rosentiel, A. K. and Keefe, F. J. (1983). The use of coping strategies in chronic low back pain: relationship to patient characteristics and current adjustment. *Pain*, 17, 33–44.

Roth, A. and Fonagy, P. (2005). *What Works for Whom? A Critical Review of Psychotherapy Research*. 2nd edition. New York: Guilford.

Roth, A. D. and Pilling, S. (2007). *The Competences Required to Deliver Effective Cognitive and Behavioural Therapy for People with Depression and with Anxiety Disorders*. London: Department of Health (available online at www.uccl.ac.uk/CORE/).

Roth, A. D., Pilling, S. and Turner, J. (2010). Therapist training and supervision in clinical trials: Implications for clinical practice. *Behavioural and Cognitive Psychotherapy*, 38, 291–302.

Sabin-Farrell, R. and Turpin, G. (2003). Vicarious traumatization: Implicatioms for the mental health of health workers? *Clinical Psychology Review*, 23, 449–80.

Safran, J. D. and Muran, J. C. (2006). Has the concept of the therapeutic alliance outlived its usefulness? *Psychotherapy, Theory, Research, Practice, Training*, 43, 286–91.

Schmidt, N. B., Salas, D., Bernert, R. and Schatschneider, C. (2005). Diagnosing agoraphobia in the context of panic disorder: Examining the effects of DSM IV criteria on diagnostic decision making. *Behaviour Research and Therapy*, 43, 1219–29.

Schultz, P. M., Resick, P. A., Huber, L. C. and Griffin, M. G. (2006). The effectiveness of cognitive processing therapy for PTSD with refugees in a community setting. *Cognitive and Behavioral Practice*, 13, 322–31.

Scott, M. J. and Stradling, S. G. (1987). Evaluation of a group programme for parents of problem children. *Behavioural Psychotherapy*, 15, 224–39.

——. (1990). Group cognitive therapy for depression produces clinically significant reliable change in community-based settings. *Behavioural Psychotherapy*, 18, 1–19.

——. (1997). Client compliance with exposure treatments for post-traumatic stress disorder. *Journal of Traumatic Stress*, 10, 523–6.

Scott, M. J. (2009). *Simply Effective Cognitive Behaviour Therapy: A practitioner's guide*. London: Routledge.

——. (2011). *Simply Effective Group Cognitive Behaviour Therapy: A practitioner's guide*. London: Routledge.

——. (2012). *CBT for Common Trauma Responses*. London: Sage Publications.

Segal, Z. V., Williams, J. M. G. and Teasdale, J. D. (2002). *Mindfulness-based Cognitive Therapy for Depression: A new approach to preventing relapse*. New York: Guilford Press.

Shafran, R., Clark, D. M., Fairburn, C. G. and Arntz, A. (2009). Mind the gap: Improving the dissemination of CBT. *Behaviour Research and Therapy*, 47, 902–9.

Shapiro, D. (2002) Renewing the scientist-practitioner model, *The Psychologist*, 15, 232–4.

Shaw, B. F., Elkin, I., Yamagughi, J., Olmsted, M., Vallis, T. M., Dobson, K. S., Lowery, A., Sotsky, S. M., Watkins, J. T. and Imber, S. D. (1999). Therapist competence ratings in relation to clinical outcome in cognitive therapy of depression. *Journal of Consulting and Clinical Psychology*, 67, 837–46.

Shear, M. K., Greeno, C., Kang, J., Ludewig, D., Frank, E., Swartz, H. A. and Hanekamp, M. (2000). Diagnosis of nonpsychotic patients in community clinics. *American Journal of Psychiatry* 157, 581–7.

Sloan, D. M., Marx, B. P., Bovin, M., Feinstein, B. A. and Gallagher, M. W. (2012). Written exposure as an intervention for PTSD: A randomized clinical trial with motor vehicle accident survivors. *Behaviour Research and Therapy*, 50, 627–35.

Sloan, G. (2005). Clinical supervision: Beginning the supervisory relationship. *British Journal of Nursing*, 14, 918–23.

Southam-Gerow, M. A., Weisz, J. R., Chu, B. C., McLeod, B. D., Gordis, E. B. and Connor-Smith, J. K. (2010). Does cognitive behavioural therapy for youth anxiety outperform usual care in community clinics? An initial effectiveness test. *Journal of the American Academy of Child and Adolescent Psychiatry*, 49, 1043–52.

Spring, B. and Neville, K. (2011). Evidence based practise in Clinical Psychology, in D. H. Barlow (ed.) *The Oxford Handbook of Clinical Psychology*, pp. 128–49. New York: Oxford University Press.

Stewart, R. E. and Chambless, D. L. (2009). Cognitive-behavioral therapy for adult anxiety disorders in clinical practice: A meta-analysis of effectiveness studies. *Journal of Consulting and Clinical Psychology*, 77, 595–606.

Stirman, S. W., DeRubeis, R. J., Crits-Christoph, P. and Rothman, A. (2005). Can the randomized controlled trial literature generalize to non-randomized patients? *Journal of Consulting and Clinical Psychology*, 73, 127–35.

Tarrier, N., Sommerfield, C., Pilgrim, H. and Humphreys, L. (1999). Cognitive therapy or imaginal exposure in the treatment of post-traumatic stress disorder. Twelve-month follow up. *British Journal of Psychiatry*, 175, 571–5.

Tarrier, N. (2001). What can be learned from clinical trials? Reply to Devilly and Foa (2001). *Journal of Consulting and Clinical Psychology*, 69, 117–18.

Townend, K., Iannetta, L. and Freeston, M. H. (2002). Clinical supervision in practice: a survey of UK cognitive behavioural psychotherapists accredited by the BABCP. *Behavioural and Cognitive Psychotherapy*, 30, 485–500.

Trepka, C., Rees, A., Shapiro, D. A., Hardy, G. E. and Barkham, M. (2004). Therapist outcome and outcome of cognitive therapy for depression. *Cognitive Therapy and Research*, 28, 143–57.

Turpin, G. and Wheeler, S. (2011). *IAPT Supervision Guidance*. Revised March 2011.

Wallbank, S. and Hatton, S. (2011). Reducing burnout and stress: the effectiveness of clinical supervision. *Community Practitioner*, 84, 21–5.

Waller, G., Corstorphine, E., Hinrichsen, H., Lawson, R., Mountford, V. and Russell, K. (2007). *Cognitive Behavioral Therapy for Eating Disorders: A Comprehensive Treatment Guide*. Cambridge University Press.

Waller, G., Stringer, H. and Meyer, C. (2012). What cognitive behavioural techniques do therapists report using when delivering cognitive behavioural therapy for eating disorders? *Journal of Consulting and Clinical Psychology*, 80, 171–5.

Wampold, B. E., Imel, Z. E., Laska, K. M. and Benish, S. (2010). Determining what works in the treatment of PTSD. *Clinical Psychology Review*, 30, 923–33.

Wampold, B. E., Budge, S. L. and Laska, K. M. (2011). Evidence-based treatments for depression and anxiety versus treatment-as-usual: A meta-analysis of direct comparisons. *Clinical Psychology Review*, 31, 1304–12.

Watkins, C. E. (2011). Does psychotherapy supervision contribute to patient outcomes? Considering thirty years of research. *The Clinical Supervisor*, 30, 235–56.

Webb, C. A., Derubeis, R. J. and Barber, J. P. (2010). Therapist adherence/competence and treatment outcome: A meta-analytic review. *Journal of Consulting and Clinical Psychology*, 78, 200–11.

Wells, A. (2009). *Metacognitive Therapy for Anxiety and Depression*. New York: Guilford Press.

Westbrook, D. and Kirk, J. (2005). The clinical effectiveness of cognitive behaviour therapy: outcome for a large sample of adults treated in routine practice. *Behaviour Research and Therapy*, 43, 1243–61.

Westen, D. and Morrison, K. (2001). A multidimensional meta-analysis of treatments for depression, panic and generalized anxiety disorder: An empirical examination of the status of empirically supported therapies. *Journal of Consulting and Clinical Psychology*, 69, 875–99.

White, E. and Winstanley, J. (2010). A randomised controlled trial of clinical supervision: Selected findings from a novel Australian attempt to establish the evidence base for causal relationships with quality of care and patient outcomes, as an informed contribution to mental health nursing practice development. *Journal of Research in Nursing*, 15, 151–67.

Wiborg, J. F., Knoop, Wensing, M. and Bleijenberg, G. (2012). Therapists effects and the dissemination of cognitive behaviour therapy for chronic fatigue syndrome in community-based mental health care. *Behaviour Research and Therapy*, 50, 393–6.

Williams, C. (2003). *Overcoming Anxiety: A five areas approach*. London: Hodder Arnold.

Young, J. E. (1994). *Cognitive Therapy for Personality Disorders: A schema-focused approach*. Revised Edition. Sarasota, FL: Professional Resource Press.

Young, J. and Beck, A. T. (1980) Cognitive Therapy rating scale: rating manual. *Unpublished Manuscript*. Philadelphia: Centre for Cognitive Therapy, University of Pennsylvania.

Zayfert, C., DeViva, J. C., Becker, C. B., Pike, J. L., Gillock, K. L. and Hayes, S. A. (2005). Exposure utilization and completion of cognitive behavioral therapy for PTSD in a 'real world' clinical practice. *Journal of Traumatic Stress*, 18, 637–45.

Zimmerman, M. and Mattia, J. I. (1999). Psychiatric diagnosis in clinical practice: Is comorbidity being missed? *Comprehensive Psychiatry* 40, 182–91.

——. (2000). Principal and additional DSM-IV disorders for which outpatients seek treatment. *Psychiatric Services* 51, 1299–304.

Index

Italic page numbers denote figures and tables